Grammar and Punctuation Guide

Del Merrick

SCHOLASTIC
New York Toronto London Auckland
Sydney New Delhi Hong Kong

Grammar and Punctuation Guide

ISBN: 978-93-5275-081-8

Author: Del Merrick
Editor: Vanessa Barker
Design and illustration: Janice Bowles

Reprinted by Scholastic India Pvt. Ltd.
A-27, Ground Floor, Sigma Centre
Infocity-1, Sector 34, Gurgaon 122001 (India)

First edition: May 2017

This reprint edition: July 2025

Printed in india at MicroPrints India, New Delhi

CONTENTS

CONTENTS continued...

HOW TO USE THIS BOOK

Grammar and Punctuation Guide has been written to help young grammar students explore and understand how our language 'works'. We speak and write in words. These are the tools of our language. We use them every day, and grammar is like the glue that holds them together. Each word has an important and specific job to do. This book will clearly explain how words work with each other to create a language that others can understand.

Each of the major sections of the book contains simple explanations about the way words are used, together with many easy-to-understand examples. These are often followed by a **TRY THIS** quiz so students can apply and test their new knowledge. Each major section concludes with a **Wrap-Up** — a summary of the information provided.

The Guide also contains a number of **Troublespots** to alert students to errors that are often made in grammar.

Grammar and Punctuation Guide also contains a detailed index to help locate specific sections quickly, and a glossary that offers a short definition and example of each grammatical term used in the book. There are further cross-references throughout the guide.

ABOUT the AUTHOR

Del has enjoyed a long career in education as a specialist teacher (Learning Difficulties), education adviser and regional coordinator (English). She has written extensively for parents, teachers and students, and is a well-known and respected author nationally and internationally. Her publications cover a diverse range of print and electronic materials for English grammar, spelling, reading, writing and comprehension. Among her latest works for primary students are *Blake's Comprehension Guide* and *Targeting Spelling*, a comprehensive spelling program.

INTRODUCTION

People use language to communicate with each other. They express themselves through **spoken** or **written language** (words), **visual language** (pictures) and **body language** (the way they use their bodies through their hands, faces and body movements).

Speaking

Speaking *(face-to-face)*

Reading

Writing

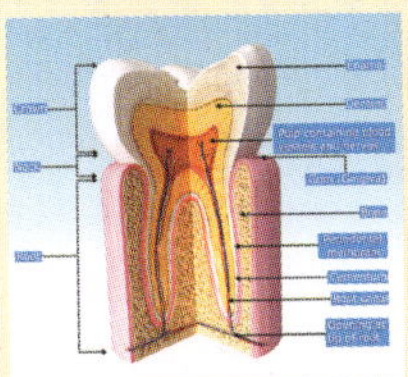

Pictures *(visual language)*

Movements *(body language)*

We think and express ourselves through language.

Through language we can:

- chat with friends
- say how we feel
- buy things
- ask questions.
- express our thoughts
- ask for what we want
- learn new things

Words are the building blocks of our language. Most people learn to use them by copying what they hear others say. They learn how to use words to make sense.

Example

I | stood | on | tip-toe | to | see | out | the | window.

NOT

I | tip-toe | stood | out | to | see | on | the | window.

Putting words together so that they make sense is the **grammar** of our language. This book will help you understand more about how our language works.

SENTENCES

A chunk containing a complete thought is called a sentence.

People express themselves in meaningful 'chunks' of language. A chunk containing a complete thought is called a sentence.

Examples

I have six goldfish.

Where did you find the key to the back door?

We play cricket in the backyard at weekends.

You'll be in real trouble if you lose your hat again!

A sentence makes sense on its own.

In **spoken language**, the sentences are spoken, with a small pause between sentences to show where they begin and end. People use their voices, hands and faces to express what they want to say.

In **written language**, each sentence begins with a capital letter and ends with a full stop, question mark or exclamation mark. There are small, white spaces between words to show where they begin and end.

Try this

Which of these chunks of language are sentences?

1. in the backyard near the garden shed
2. We went for a ride on the merry-go-round at the Royal Show.
3. Ash from the volcano fell on the village.
4. down the long, dusty road
5. It looks like rain, so you will need to take an umbrella.

Remember, a sentence is a complete thought!

STATEMENTS

Some sentences are **statements**. They tell listeners or readers about everyday things, facts and ideas.

Examples

We went to visit our uncle last Sunday.

Everyone should wear a hat at the beach.

Eva is captain of the netball team.

The wind blew my umbrella away.

I think we should go home soon.

A **full stop** is placed at the end of a written statement.

Examples

I play games with my friends.

It is cold in winter.

I gave mum a bunch of roses.

A statement can be a **fact** or an **opinion**.

Fact: Something that is true. *Australia is an island. The sun sets in the west.*

Opinion: What someone thinks about something. *Apples are nicer than oranges.*

Try this

Are these statements of fact or opinion?

1. There are too many programs on TV for kids.
2. A koala is a native Australian animal.
3. Everyone should learn how to swim.
4. A violin is played with a bow.
5. A torch gives more light than a lantern.

QUESTIONS

Some sentences are **questions**. An answer is usually expected.

Examples

Where have you been?

Are there any biscuits left?

Have you all eaten your lunch?

Do you know how to play chess?

Have you seen a blue butterfly?

A **question mark** is placed at the end of a written question.

Examples

What time does this bus leave?

Can you swim?

What class are you in?

The sound of our voice rises and falls as we speak. This is called **pitch**, and it can be low or high. In spoken language, we usually raise the pitch of our voice a little at the end of the sentence.

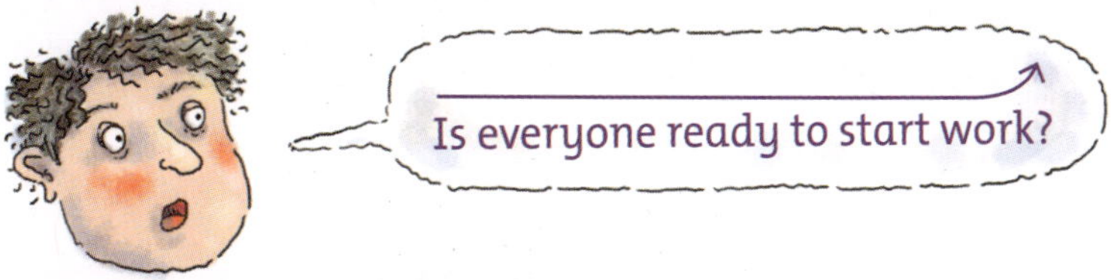

Answers to spoken questions are usually statements. Sometimes they are not complete sentences, but are understood by both speakers.

Example

SENTENCES

EXCLAMATIONS

Some sentences are **exclamations** to show sudden surprise or fear, happiness or excitement.

Examples

Look! There's a snake!
Thank you for my gift. Thank you! Thank you!
Hurry, Jen, there's a storm coming!
I can't wait until Friday!
Go inside, immediately!

An **exclamation mark** is placed at the end of a written exclamation.

Examples

He was late for school, again!
What a fabulous bike!
Get out of the way!

In **spoken language**, the important words are spoken loudly.

In **written language**, whole words may be written in **capital letters** to show how the writer is feeling.

Examples

Get inside, NOW! (angry)
WOW! I don't know what to say! (surprised)
You're my BEST friend! (happy)
HELP! My boat is sinking! (scared)

COMMANDS

Some sentences are **commands**. They request or demand that the listener or reader do something. They begin with a **doing verb**. (See Verbs p. 39)

Examples

Throw the ball to Jack.
Wait for me, please.
Cook the eggs for three minutes.
Colour the apples red.
Kick the ball as far as you can.

A **full stop** is placed at the end of a written command.

A command sometimes ends with an **exclamation mark**.

Examples

Run to the fence and back.
Fill the bucket with water.
Go to bed, NOW!

A sentence always has a subject and a verb.

SUBJECT AND PREDICATE

A sentence has two parts:

1. a **subject** that tells you **who** or **what** the sentence is about
2. a **predicate** that tells you what the subject is **doing**. The predicate always has a **verb**. (See Verbs p. 39)

Examples

Subject	Predicate
My brother and I	*play cricket on Saturdays.*
She	*likes green jelly and ice cream.*
The red and yellow kite	*floated high above the tree tops.*
The fishing boats	*will return to shore at sunset.*
Lots of people	*are watching the soccer game.*

Verb (play) … *Verb* (are watching)

SUBJECT-VERB AGREEMENT (See Verbs p. 42)

A **singular subject** names **one** thing. *A fat, little **pig** ...*

A **plural subject** names **more than one** thing. *All the **children** ...*

A singular subject has a **singular verb**.

A fat, little pig is rolling in the mud.

A plural subject has a **plural verb**.
All the children are feeding the ducks.

SUBJECT AND OBJECT

All sentences have a **subject**. Some sentences also have an **object**.

The subject **does** the action and the object **receives** the action. The object usually follows the **verb**.

Example

*Gus dropped **the ball**.*

subject ↑ (Gus) verb ↑ (dropped) object ↑ (the ball)

The object answers the question 'what' after the verb.

Examples

*My brother downloads **music** from the web.*

*William gave **the cricket bat** to the next player.*

Try this

What are the subjects and objects in these sentences?

1. Mum put a bowl of soup in front of me.
2. Ben and his friends are playing chess in the library.
3. The female magpie builds her nest high up in the fork of a tree.
4. Every morning and afternoon, the farmer milks the cows.
5. Jan baked a chocolate cake for afternoon tea.

SIMPLE SENTENCES

A **simple sentence** has a subject and a verb.

The big bus stopped at the school gate.
We shivered in the cold, damp cave.
The hen and her chick are pecking at the seeds.

Examples

The subject is not always at the beginning of the sentence.

After school, Kev and Bill go to football training.
Can you swim?
What time does the library open?
Will you count all the books, please?
In a few weeks' time, the Australian swimming team will fly to Japan.

Examples

What is the subject of each sentence?

1. The sun is shining brightly today.
2. Would you like an orange?
3. Before school, I feed my pet fish.
4. A big, silver plane landed on the runway.
5. There, at the door, stood my best friend.

Try this

The subject is not always in a sentence. In a command, it is understood that **you** are the person being asked to do something. It is understood that **you** are the subject of the sentence.

(you) Clean your teeth.
(you) Stay here with your brother.
(you) Stand behind your chair.
(you) Paint the fence green.
(you) Fold the paper in half.

Examples

In commands, it is understood that you are the subject.

COMPOUND SENTENCES

Two simple sentences are joined together to make a **compound sentence**.

They are joined with a **joining word**.

And, **but**, **or** and **so** are all joining words.

Examples

Dan has a new cricket bat.	**and**	Jane has a new sports bag.

Dan has a new cricket bat and Jane has a new sports bag.

I like peaches and plums.	**but**	Lara likes apples and oranges.

I like peaches and plums, but Lara likes apples and oranges.

Do you want to read a book?	**or**	Do you want to play chess?

Do you want to read a book, or do you want to play chess?

The children were hungry.	**so**	Mum gave them some fruit.

The children were hungry, so Mum gave them some fruit.

Try this

Join these simple sentences to make compound sentences.

1. Would you like an orange? Would you like an apple?
2. I would like to buy this hat. It costs too much.
3. You make the toast. I'll cook the eggs.
4. It rained last night. The grass is very wet.
5. Harry went to the gym. William went with him.

SENTENCE WRAP-UP

Sentence	A 'chunk' of language containing one complete thought. *(I am hungry.)*
Sentence markers	A sentence begins with a capital letter and ends with a full stop **(.)**, a question mark **(?)** or an exclamation mark **(!)**.
Statements	Sentences that state facts or ideas. Statements end with a full stop. *(The sun is hot. Eva has a black horse.)*
Fact or opinion	Statements may state **facts**. *(A dingo is a wild dog.)* Statements may state **opinions**, which say what one person thinks. They may not be true. *(Children watch too much TV.)*
Questions	Sentences that ask questions. Questions end with a question mark. *(Can you swim? Do you like pizza?)*
Exclamations	Sentences that show sudden surprise, fear, happiness or excitement. Exclamations end with an exclamation mark. *(Go away! Run for cover! Help! What! You've lost your shoes!)*
Commands	Sentences that give an order or a command. It is understood that **you** are being spoken to. Commands end with a full stop. (*Cut out the map. Glue it in your book. Colour it in.)*
Subject and predicate	A sentence has two parts: 1. A subject that says who or what the sentence is about. 2. A **predicate** (the rest of the sentence) that says what the subject is doing. *(A helicopter **flew over the sea**. The pilot **was looking for a lost boat**.)*
Subject-verb agreement	A singular subject has a **singular verb**. *(The dog **is** old.)* A plural subject has a **plural verb**. (*The dogs **are** old.)*
Subject and object	A subject does the action. An **object** receives the action. *(The boy threw **a bone** to his dog. The girls are riding **bikes**.)*
Simple sentences	Have a subject and a **verb**. *(The bus **stopped** at the gate. We **cheered** for our favourite team.)*
Compound sentences	Are made up of two simple sentences joined by a **joining word**. The joining words are **and**, **but**, **or** and **so**. *(Dan has the bat **and** Joe has the ball. I wanted to go, **but** my mum said no. Will you read a book, **or** will you watch TV? It is raining, **so** we'll have to play inside.)*

WORDS

Words are the building blocks of a **sentence**.
They are put together in small 'chunks' of meaning.

Example

After school	Sue and Jill	go	to the library.
	↑ Subject	↑ Verb	

A sentence is made up of words. Each word has a job to do in the sentence.

Example

Subject: The big horse — Predicate: jumped over the gate.

The	big	horse	jumped	over	the	gate.
Article	Adjective *(describing)*	Noun *(naming)*	Verb *(doing)*	Preposition *(position)*	Article	Noun *(naming)*

Through words people find answers to these questions:

Who? What? When? Where? Why? Which? How?

NOUNS

Nouns name the things people talk and write about. They are important words that hold the key to meaning. They inform the reader who the people are and what things are involved.

Nouns name people, places, animals and things.

The boys entered the cave. Jack switched on his torch and shone the light around the rocky walls. The boys moved from cave to cave through long, dark tunnels. Suddenly, Jack stopped. Ahead of them, hundreds of green rocks lay scattered across the floor, sparkling in the torchlight. They filled their backpacks with the strange rocks.

Example

Nouns help readers make pictures in their minds.

COMMON NOUNS

Common nouns are everyday words used to name people, animals, places and things. They begin with a small letter, unless they are at the beginning of a sentence.

Examples

People	*Animals*	*Places*	*Things*
boy	*cow*	*shop*	*car*
friend	*dog*	*school*	*leaf*
actor	*elephant*	*home*	*clock*
children	*magpie*	*park*	*violin*
sister	*chicken*	*café*	*book*

Nouns express number: one, two, three, four, five, six ...

COUNT NOUNS

Count nouns are the names of things that can be counted. They name **one** thing *(cat, horse, plum, bag)* or **more than one** thing (*beds, hats, pigs, spoons*).

MASS NOUNS

Mass nouns are the names of things that **cannot** be counted (*wheat, pasta, butter, flour, sand, snow, water*). A mass noun is always followed by a **singular verb**.

COMPOUND NOUNS

Compound nouns are two nouns **joined together** to make one word.

sea	+	shell	=	seashell
pan	+	cake	=	pancake

Try this

Find the compound nouns in these sentences.

1. There was a thunderstorm last weekend.
2. Jimmy plays softball and Jessie plays netball.
3. Tim had a milkshake and a bag of popcorn.
4. Ava put toothpaste on her toothbrush.
5. He rode through the farmyard on horseback.

NUMBER (SINGULAR AND PLURAL NOUNS)

A **singular noun** names **one** thing.
A **plural noun** names **more than one** thing.

Examples

cup *cups*

bag *bags*

jug *jugs*

rose *roses*

Plurals are formed by adding **s** or **es** to the singular noun.

Add **s** most of the time.

Examples

horse	*horses*
bike	*bikes*
hand	*hands*
toy	*toys*

Plurals are formed by adding s most of the time.

Add **es** to nouns ending in **s**, **ss**, **x**, **ch** and **sh**.

Examples

bus	*buses*
dress	*dresses*
box	*boxes*
peach	*peaches*
dish	*dishes*

Add s or es to form plurals.

bone ___	pig ___	brush ___	kiss ___
fox ___	horse ___	basket ___	beach ___
trumpet ___	game ___	teacher ___	orange ___
gas ___	bunch ___	carrot ___	box ___

Try this

For nouns ending in y:

If there is a vowel before the **y**, add **s**.

Examples

boy	*boys*
day	*days*
monkey	*monkeys*

If there is a consonant before the **y**, change the **y** to **i** and add **es**.

Examples

baby	*babies*
lady	*ladies*
fairy	*fairies*

For nouns ending in f:

If you hear a **v** sound in the plural noun, change the **f** to **v** and add **es**.

Examples

shelf	*shelves*
wolf	*wolves*
calf	*calves*

If you hear an **f** sound in the plural noun, add **s**.

Examples

roof	*roofs*
dwarf	*dwarfs*
reef	*reefs*

IRREGULAR NOUNS

The **plural** form of some nouns is a different word altogether. These are called **irregular nouns**.

Examples

foot	*feet*
tooth	*teeth*
mouse	*mice*
person	*people*
man	*men*

Some nouns are both singular and plural. *(sheep, deer, fish)*

Mass nouns are only singular. *(news, wheat, gravel, bread)*

Some nouns are only plural. *(scissors, trousers, eyeglasses)*

Try this

What are the plural forms of these nouns?

gully	________	kite	________	match	________	loaf	________
train	________	path	________	woman	________	shoe	________
elf	________	goose	________	half	________	key	________

PROPER NOUNS

Proper nouns are the names of particular people, places, objects and events (*Kate, China, April, Perth, Mr Adams, Kmart, Yarra River*).
(See Capital letters p. 68)

A proper noun always begins with a capital letter.

Which words are proper nouns?

1. We sang *Waltzing Matilda* on Australia Day.
2. In March, Bob is going camping in the Snowy Mountains.
3. Mr Brown drove to Cairns in his Holden car.
4. Mrs Smith does her shopping at Woolworths every Friday.
5. David Morris won a silver medal at the Winter Olympics in Sochi.

Try this

POSSESSIVE NOUNS

Possessive nouns show ownership.
An **apostrophe** shows who the owner is.
(See Punctuation p. 72–73)

Examples

*Jack's cat (Jack is the **owner** of the cat.)*
*A hen's egg (The hen is the **owner** of the egg.)*

For **singular nouns**, place **'s** after the owner, like this:

's

The clown shoes are red.

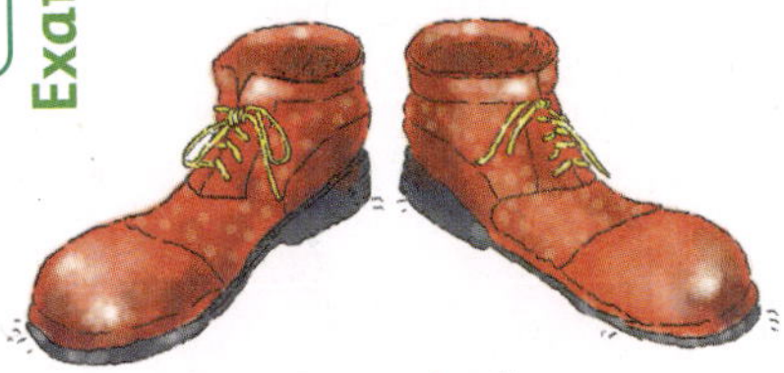

The clown's shoes are red.

Examples

a dog's collar | *a friend's bike*
mum's slippers | *the teacher's voice*

For **plural nouns**, place **'** after the owner, like this:

'

Butterflies wings are very colourful.

Butterflies' wings are very colourful.

Examples

several birds' nests | *the actors' costumes*
the brothers' bikes | *babies' photos*

Chloe likes reading children's books.

For **irregular plural nouns**, place **'s** after the owner, like this:

Chloe likes reading children['s] books.

Examples

women's clothing	*people's voices*
mice's nests	*men's shoes*

TROUBLESPOT

An apostrophe is used with possessive nouns NOT plural nouns.

✓ The trucks are going down the hill.

✗ The truck's are going down the hill.

Find the possessive nouns below. Are they singular or plural?

1. Mum's books and Dad's eyeglasses were on the table.
2. All we saw were rabbits' tails disappearing down the burrow.
3. Spiders' webs sparkled in the sun's rays.
4. The athletes' tracksuits are green and gold.
5. Magpies' nests are made from twigs, sticks and grasses.

Try this

COLLECTIVE NOUNS

Collective nouns are names given to groups of people, animals and things.

Examples

a flock of birds	*a mob of emus*
a crowd of people	*a nest of tables*
a herd of cows	*a pod of whales*

Collective nouns are **singular nouns**. When they are the subject of a sentence, they are followed by a **singular verb**. (See Subject-verb agreement p. 6)

Examples

A mob of kangaroos ***is drinking*** *at the waterhole.*

The flock of seagulls ***is flying*** *over the fishing boats.*

A pack of wolves ***gathers*** *in the hills.*

GENDER NOUNS

Sometimes we use particular nouns to name males and females (boys and girls). These are called **gender nouns**.

Examples

Male	*Female*
man	*woman*
bull	*cow*
king	*queen*

Many nouns can be either male or female.

Examples

author *athlete* *teacher*
doctor *singer* *lawyer*

Most things are neither male nor female.

Examples

rose *leaf* *moon*
carrot *trumpet* *shop*
house *ball* *chair*

Try this

Sort the nouns into their correct gender groups of either 'male', 'female', 'male or female', or 'neither male nor female'.

princess	planet	rooster	uncle
wheat	driver	grandma	car
hero	lady	foal	father
mare	baby	prince	book

NOUN GROUPS

A **noun group** is a group of words. The **noun** is the main word.

Examples

an old friend *lots of apples*
the red bike *a big, sleepy, tabby cat*

Noun groups help people picture things in their minds.

The words that say more about the noun come before it.

Examples

a strange dream
a faithful friend
dark storm clouds
Jack's new shoes
a spelling problem
sparkling raindrops
thirty children
china teacups
some people

Find the noun groups in these sentences.

1. A strong wind is blowing away the grey clouds.
2. Chop up two red tomatoes and grate some cheese.
3. We watched an exciting football game yesterday.
4. Heavy rain fell overnight.
5. One man is playing a silver trumpet.

Try this

ARTICLES

The words **a**, **an** and **the** come before nouns. These words are called **articles**. They are often the first word in a **noun group**.

Examples

a bag of potatoes
an angry bull
the tallest boy in the class.

the

the relates to a particular person or thing.
the tells people **who** or **what** is being spoken about.
the is called the **definite article**.

the comes before singular and plural nouns.

Examples

Put the lid back on the box.

It is the last day of school!

The boys in the red team won the game.

The children went to see the lions and the tigers at the zoo.

The farmer's dog chased the cows around the paddock.

a and **an** do not relate to any particular person or thing.

a is used before a singular noun *(a tall ship, a magpie, a wrong answer).*

an is used before a singular noun beginning with a vowel *(an egg, an old horse, an eye).*

a and **an** are called **indefinite articles**.

Examples

Take an umbrella if it rains.

Put on a hat before you go outside.

Break an egg into a cup and add a teaspoon of water.

I need a new pair of sunglasses and some sunscreen.

I bought some butter, some bread and some apples.

The word some is used before plural nouns and mass nouns.

Use **a** when you introduce a person or thing for the first time. Use **the** as you continue to talk about that person or thing.

Example

Bee is lying very still on a ledge below the cliff. Benson grabs a rope and ties it to a rock. He throws the rope over the edge.
"Grab the rope, Bee, and I'll pull you up," Benson shouts.
As he lifts Bee over the ledge to safety, the rock gives way and tumbles over the edge.

NOUN WRAP-UP

Common nouns	Name people, places, animals and things. *(boy, river, fox, chair)*
Count nouns	Name things that **can be counted**. *(plum, bag, hat, spoon)*
Mass nouns	Name things that **can't be counted**. *(snow, rain, sand)*
Compound nouns	Nouns made up of **two words**. *(seaside, popcorn, cupcake)*
Singular nouns	Name **one** thing. *(cup, bed, car, bike)*
Plural nouns	Name **more than one** thing. Plural nouns are formed by adding **s** or **es** to the noun. *(flowers, chickens, buses)*
Proper nouns	Name particular people, places, objects and events. They begin with a **capital letter**. *(David, Sydney, Eiffel Tower, Olympic Games)*
Possessive nouns	Name the owner of something. An **apostrophe** is used to show ownership. **Singular:** *Jack's bike, the man's car, my friend's mum* **Plural:** *foxes' den, riders' horses, hens' eggs*
Collective nouns	Name groups of people, animals and things. *(a **crowd** of people, a **flock** of birds, a **nest** of tables)*
Noun groups	A group of words with a noun as the main word. *(an old and very fat **pig**; the long, winding **road**; a good **book**)*
Articles	The articles **a**, **an** and **the** are used to introduce nouns. *(**a** cloudy day, **an** elephant, **the** cat, **the** big house)*

ADJECTIVES

Adjectives describe and give meaning to nouns.

Adjectives are words used to describe people, places and things in a particular way.

They work with the **noun** to create a particular meaning. They build clear pictures in the mind of the reader or listener.

DESCRIBING

Adjectives describe:

size — *big truck, long hair, tall man, little mouse*
shape — *round table, square box, oval frame*
colour — *red shorts, blue sky, yellow moon*
sound — *loud knock, soft voice, noisy parrots*
feeling — *happy children, sleepy baby, angry boy*
qualities — *kind face, wonderful day, untidy room*
number — *seven cats, many days, twenty dollars, few friends.*

Adjectives add details about the noun.

Adjectives are often part of a **noun group**. (See Noun groups pp. 17–18)

One or more adjectives can be used to describe the noun.

Adjectives can come **before** the noun as part of a noun group.

Examples

There are small, black ants in the kitchen!

The sweetest and juiciest fruit is at the top of the tree.

I bought a dozen sticky buns at the shop.

Five girls and seven boys are waiting for a bus.

I used red, blue and yellow paper to make a colourful kite.

Adjectives answer three questions about nouns: What kind? How many? Which one?

Adjectives can come **after** the noun.

Try this

Examples

Jill's hat is bright red and her coat is yellow.
The river is long and wide.
That box looks heavy.
The sky looks pretty at sunset.
Her hair is long and brown.

Find the adjectives that describe the underlined nouns.

1. A large parcel came in the mail.
2. Ken has dark brown eyes.
3. After a few months, Sally had enough money to buy new shoes.
4. The golden coach was pulled by six white horses.
5. Dan was the first person to cross the finishing line.

ADJECTIVE PHRASES

Adjective phrases follow the noun. They answer the question which about the noun.

An **adjective phrase** is a group of words that does the work of an **adjective**.
It tells you **which** person, place or thing is being spoken about. It **follows** the noun and often begins with a **preposition**. (See Preposition phrases pp. 62–63)

Examples

The boy in the red shirt won the chess competition.
The books on the table belong to Sam.
We all wanted the chocolates in the gold wrappers.
The captain of the team scored the first goal.
All the birds in the cage belong to Mrs Black.

Try this

Find the adjective phrases that describe the underlined nouns.

1. The clothes on the line are nearly dry.
2. A boy with a note came to the door of our classroom.
3. He looked closely at the photo on the wall.
4. You will need to bring a box of spare batteries.
5. The sheep in the top paddock will soon be shorn.

PARTICIPLES (PRESENT AND PAST)

(See Verbs pp. 46–47)

Present participles end in **–ing**. They can be used as adjectives. These adjectives are often called **verbal adjectives**.

Examples

He has a walking stick.
We swam in the sparkling water.
He told us an amazing story.
Mum put clothes in the washing machine.
It was hard to see in the fading light.

A verbal adjective ends in –ing or –ed and describes a noun.

Past participles end in **–ed**. They can be used as adjectives. These adjectives are often called **verbal adjectives**.

Examples

He wore a crumpled jacket.
I milked the spotted cow.
Ben was wearing a striped shirt.
There are potted plants on our verandah.
We had sliced tomatoes and grated cheese.

Be careful! Verbal adjectives look like verbs, but do the work of adjectives.

Find the verbal adjectives in these sentences. Remember, verbal adjectives describe a noun.

1. I am wearing my new swimming costume.
2. I like steamed vegetables and baked potatoes.
3. He carried a lighted candle.
4. There was a surprised look on his face.
5. A man is fishing in the flowing river.

Try this

ANTONYMS

Adjectives describe things in opposite ways. These 'opposite' words are called **antonyms**.

Examples

A man can be tall or short.
Clouds can be high or low.
Oranges can be sweet or sour.

Here are some antonyms that people often use.

old and new	*fast and slow*	*long and short*	*left and right*
wet and dry	*old and young*	*fresh and stale*	*big and little*
hard and soft	*right and wrong*	*wild and tame*	*fat and thin*

ADJECTIVE SUFFIXES

A suffix is a syllable added to the end of a word.

A **suffix** is a syllable attached to the end of a word to change the way the word is used. Some adjectives can be formed by adding an **adjective suffix** to another word.

Examples

Adding ***–y***		*Adding* ***–able***		*Adding* ***–ous***	
stick	*sticky*	*comfort*	*comfortable*	*fame*	*famous*
dust	*dusty*	*like*	*likeable*	*danger*	*dangerous*
sand	*sandy*	*use*	*useable*	*venom*	*venomous*
bump	*bumpy*	*port*	*portable*	*nerve*	*nervous*
fun	*funny*	*wear*	*wearable*	*fury*	*furious*
mud	*muddy*	*break*	*breakable*	*glory*	*glorious*

Adding the suffixes **–ful** and **–less** makes antonyms (words of opposite meaning).

Remember, –ful = full of and –less = without.

Examples

	Adding –ful	***Adding –less***
use	*useful*	*useless*
power	*powerful*	*powerless*
harm	*harmful*	*harmless*

Create antonyms by adding -ful and -less to these words.

1. hope ____________ful ____________less
2. care ____________ ____________
3. thought ____________ ____________
4. rest ____________ ____________
5. help ____________ ____________

Try this

ADJECTIVES OF DEGREE

Adjectives show how people and things compare with each other. These adjectives are called **adjectives of degree**. They are made by adding the suffixes **-er** and **-est** to an adjective.

Examples

a big rock, a bigger rock, the biggest rock
a long rope, a longer rope, the longest rope
a tall boy, a taller boy, the tallest boy

To create adjectives of degree:

* add **-er** to compare **two** things
* add **-est** to compare **more than two** things.

Examples

Adjective	Add -er	Add -est
loud	louder	loudest
soft	softer	softest
wide	wider	widest
fine	finer	finest
low	lower	lowest

Adjective	Add -er	Add -est
safe	safer	safest
noisy	noisier	noisiest
sharp	sharper	sharpest
sad	sadder	saddest
small	smaller	smallest

Remember, there are some exceptions to these rules:

good	better	best
bad	worse	worst
many	more	most
little	less	least

sad sadder saddest

Add -er or -est to complete the adjectives correctly.

1. Brian is the young ____ boy in our class.
2. I can run fast ____ than you!
3. Who is old ____, Ben or Bella?
4. The sweet ____ fruit is at the top of the tree.
5. My hair is short, but I think yours is short ____.

Try this

If an adjective already has a suffix, adjectives of degree are created by placing **more** and **most** before the adjective. Use **more** to compare **two** things. Use **most** to compare **more than two**.

Examples

*a care**ful** person*	*a more careful person*	*the most careful person*
*a fam**ous** person*	*a more famous person*	*the most famous person*
*an act**ive** person*	*a more active person*	*the most active person*

Try this

Add more or most before the adjectives of degree.

1. My chair is ____________ comfortable than yours.
2. You are the ____________ helpful person I know.
3. Some spiders are ____________ dangerous than others.
4. A knife is my ____________ useful kitchen tool.
5. Australia has some of the ____________ venomous snakes in the world.

ADJECTIVE WRAP-UP

Adjectives	Describe a noun. *(**long** hair, **rosy** cheeks, **tall** man, **kind** face, **two** girls)* They can come **before** a noun. *(the **lost** shoe, my **red** and **green** hat)* They can come **after** the noun. *(The box was **heavy**. My coat is **thick** and **warm**)*
Adjective phrases	Groups of words that do the work of adjectives. An adjective phrase directly follows a noun. It answers the question **which** about the noun. *(the boy **with the red hair**, the clothes **on the line**)*
Verbal adjectives	Present and past participles used as adjectives. *(a **walking** stick, **falling** snow, a **puzzled** look, **baked** beans, a **hidden** cave, a **broken** leg)*
Antonyms	Words that are **opposite** in meaning. *(big, little; fast, slow; wet, dry; cold, hot)*
Suffixes	Word endings. The suffixes **–y**, **–ful**, **–less**, **–ous** and **–able** form adjectives. *(dust**y**, curl**y**, help**ful**, use**ful**, danger**ous**, fam**ous**, comfort**able**, like**able**)*
Adjectives of degree	Adjectives that show how people or things compare with each other: To compare **two** things, add **–er**. *(I am **bigger** than you and **taller** and **smarter**.)* To compare **more than two** things, add **–est**. *(This piece of rope is the **longest** and the **thickest**.)* If an adjective already has a suffix: To compare **two** things, place **more** before the adjective. *(**more** careful, **more** useless)* To compare **more than two** things, place **most** before the adjective. *(**most** famous, **most** active)*

Pronouns replace the names of people and things.

PRONOUNS

Pronouns are words that are used to replace nouns *(John = he, Bella = she, boys = they).*

PERSONAL PRONOUNS

Personal pronouns replace the names of people and things. Like nouns, they can be singular or plural.

Singular pronouns replace **singular nouns**.
Plural pronouns replace **plural nouns**.

Singular		*Plural*	
I	*me*	*we*	*us*
he	*him*	*they*	*them*
she	*her*	*you*	
you	*it*		

Some pronouns come **before the verb** (the **subject** of a sentence).

Pronouns before the verb:

I he she we they you it

Examples

I ***like*** *chocolate.*

We ***went*** *to the movies.*

You ***swim*** *well.*

They ***won*** *the cricket match.*

She ***rides*** *horses.*

He ***plays*** *soccer.*

It ***is*** *a wonderful day.*

Some pronouns come **after the verb** (the **object** of a sentence). (See Subject and object p. 6)

Pronouns after the verb:

me him her us them you it

Examples

Give me your raincoat.
Mum kissed her on the cheek.
Tom saw him in the park yesterday.
The teacher showed us a map of Australia.
Dad told them to wait for the next bus.
I love you.

The pronoun **you** can be both singular and plural, and can come before or after the verb.
The pronoun **it** can also be placed anywhere in a sentence.

Examples

You are my best friend.
I can help you lift that box.
I have a pet bird. It is a talking parrot.
Jen has a dog. She takes it for a walk every day.

TROUBLESPOT

Be careful which pronoun you use before and after the verb.

✔ You and I like swimming.
✘ You and me like swimming.

✔ The coach wants you and me to play in the team.
✘ The coach wants you and I to play in the team.

PERSON

The way **personal pronouns** are used to show who is speaking is called **person**. Personal pronouns fall into three groups. Some personal pronouns are used **before** the verb and some are used **after** the verb.

Before the verb (subject):

FIRST PERSON	SECOND PERSON	THIRD PERSON
The person speaking	*Person(s) speaking to each other*	*The person(s) spoken about*
I we	you	he she they it

After the verb (object):

FIRST PERSON	SECOND PERSON	THIRD PERSON
The person speaking	*Person(s) speaking to each other*	*The person(s) spoken about*
me us	you	him her them it

A writer uses **first person pronouns** to tell a personal story.

Example

Last weekend, I went with Jack to watch the Rodeo Reds play in the football Grand Final. Billy came with us. We had front row seats, so we could see all the action up close. The Rodeo Reds are our favourite team, and we cheered loudly every time they scored a goal.

A writer uses **second person pronouns** when people are speaking to each other.

Example

"Tyson, you need to hurry! Have you packed your lunch?" Mum asked.

"Not yet, Mum," Tyson replied.

"You must hurry. The bus will be here soon. Get your books and your bag," Mum said.

"Okay. Do you know where my hat is?" Tyson asked.

A writer uses **third person pronouns** when speaking about other people and things.

Example

The circus parade had begun. The ringmaster came first. He waved his black top hat at the crowd. The clowns then came behind him in their baggy pants and red noses. They rode unicycles and did cartwheels. They were followed by five trotting horses with acrobats on their backs.

Try this

Are these sentences written in first, second or third person?

1. We are going to New Zealand for our holidays.
2. Did you go to the zoo with your friends on Saturday?
3. I asked Joe to come to the library with me.
4. Mr Jones took his children to visit their grandmother.
5. The teacher gave them red pens to mark their work.

POSSESSIVE PRONOUNS

Like nouns, **possessive pronouns** show ownership.
Like nouns they can be **singular** or **plural**.
Unlike nouns, they **do not** need an apostrophe.

Singular		*Plural*	
my	*mine*	*our*	*ours*
your	*yours*	*your*	*yours*
her	*hers*	*their*	*theirs*
his	*its*		

Examples

Here is my book.
That hat is mine.
Put on your coat, Jack.
This toy is yours, Sam.
Jan spoke to her brother.
This ball is hers.
Dan is his best friend.

We gave our books to the teacher.
The bikes are ours.
Give me your homework.
Is this football yours?
The riders put on their helmets.
These clothes are theirs.
The cat licks its paws.

TROUBLESPOT

Don't confuse it's and its.

it's:
is a contraction
is a pronoun + verb (it is)
is the subject of a sentence.

✔ It's going to rain soon.
✘ Its going to rain soon.

its:
is a possessive pronoun
comes before a noun.

✔ The cat licks its paws.
✘ The cat licks it's paws.

TROUBLESPOT

Don't confuse you're and your.

you're:
is a contraction
is a pronoun + verb (you are)
is the subject of a sentence.

✔ You're my best friend.
✘ Your my best friend.

your:
is a possessive pronoun
comes before a noun.

✔ Put on your hat, Jim.
✘ Put on you're hat, Jim.

Add a possessive pronoun to complete each sentence.

1. John lost ______ shoe.
2. Sue found the dollar, so it is ______.
3. They put on ______ gum boots.
4. Did you clean ______ teeth before bed?
5. This ball has my name on it, so it is ______.

Try this

REFLEXIVE PRONOUNS

Reflexive pronouns refer to the subject of the sentence.

Singular	*Plural*
myself	*ourselves*
yourself	*yourselves*
himself	*themselves*
herself	
itself	

Examples

Mr Brown bought himself a set of golf clubs.
I saw myself in the mirror.
Mary enjoyed herself at the school dance.
One horse is standing by itself in the paddock.
The boys made a tree house all by themselves.

Add a reflexive pronoun to complete each sentence.

1. I could do it ______ if I tried.
2. Jake can climb the ladder by ______.
3. Go and do it ______!
4. She scratched ______ on the rose bush.
5. They are playing in the park by ______.

Try this

INTERROGATIVE PRONOUNS

Interrogative pronouns are used to ask questions.

who what which whose

Examples

Who is your friend?
What is your name?
Which house do you live in?
Whose coat is this?

Add an interrogative pronoun to complete each sentence.

1. ______ is your favourite fruit?
2. ______ pencil is this?
3. ______ shirt should I wear — the red one or the blue one?
4. ______ is your teacher?
5. ______ games do you like to play?

DEMONSTRATIVE PRONOUNS

Some pronouns are like shortcuts. They point to things, but don't name them. They are often used by speakers, who can point to real objects. These are called **demonstrative pronouns**.

Singular		*Plural*	
this	*that*	*these*	*those*

Examples

INDEFINITE PRONOUNS

Indefinite pronouns don't replace the names of particular people and things. They refer to them in a **general** way.

Singular		
someone	*somebody*	*something*
anyone	*anybody*	*anything*
no-one	*nobody*	*nothing*
everyone	*everybody*	*everything*

Examples

Has anyone been to the skate park?
Can somebody help me?
I saw something in the shadows.
There's nothing left to eat.
Everybody is wearing a red T-shirt.

Try this

Add an indefinite pronoun to complete each sentence.

1. Does __________ know how to make a paper plane?
2. I opened the door, but there was __________ there.
3. __________ in the team wears blue shirts and white shorts.
4. I gave the stray dog __________ to eat.
5. Can __________ tell me where the pet shop is?

PRONOUN REFERENCE

A pronoun should clearly refer to the noun it replaces. This is called **pronoun reference**.

Example

The boy has a dog. He calls her Bella.

The pronoun must agree with the noun in **number** (singular or plural).

Example

✗ *Everybody must wait for their turn to bat.*

✓ *Everybody must wait for his or her turn to bat.*

The pronoun must agree with the noun in **person** (first, second, third).

Example

✗ *Billy and I had front row seats, so they could see all the action up close.*

✓ *Billy and I had front row seats, so we could see all the action up close.*

Don't be vague about what the pronoun refers to.

Example

✗ *They say it's going to rain.*

✓ *The weathermen say it's going to rain.*

A pronoun cannot refer to a **possessive noun**.
(See Possessive nouns pp. 15–16)

Example

✗ *In the captain's speech, he was very inspiring.*

✓ *The captain's speech was very inspiring.*

Pronouns can refer **backwards** and **forwards** to nouns.

Examples

Dave met his friend Charlie at the beach.

They went surfing together.

"Will you come to the art gallery with me, Sally?" said Kay.

"Oh, yes. I would like to come with you," Sally answered.

The pronouns are in bold. What nouns do they refer to?

1. Gemma sat **her** teddy bear on the bed. **She** had put a funny hat on **its** head.
2. Jarrod and **his** brother have many toys. **They** like to play with **them** after school.
3. "Have **you** done **your** homework yet, David?"
4. "What have **you** done with **my** bat, Gerry?" Joe asked, glaring at **him**.
5. Stan and I gave some lollies to **our** friends. **They** thanked **us** for sharing **them**.

Try this

PRONOUN WRAP-UP

Personal	Singular subject	I, he, she, you, it
	Plural subject	we, they, you
	Singular object	me, him, her, you, it
	Plural object	us, them, you
Person	First person subject	I, we
	First person object	me, us
	Second person subject	you
	Second person object	you
	Third person subject	he, she, they, it
	Third person object	him, her, them, it
Possessive	Singular	my, mine, your, yours, her, hers, his, its
	Plural	our, ours, your, yours, their, theirs
Reflexive	Singular	myself, yourself, himself, herself, itself
	Plural	ourselves, yourselves, themselves
Interrogative	Questions	who, what, which, whose
Demonstrative	Singular	this, that
	Plural	these, those
Indefinite	Singular	someone, somebody, something, anyone, anybody, anything, no-one, nobody, nothing, everyone, everybody, everything
Pronoun reference	A pronoun should refer to the nouns it replaces and must agree with the noun in number. Pronouns can refer backwards and forwards to nouns. (*"Will* ***you*** *come to the park with* ***me****,* ***Kay****?" asked* ***Sally****. "Yes.* ***I*** *would like to come with* ***you****,"* ***she*** *said.)*	

VERBS

Verbs tell us what is 'going on' in a sentence.

Every sentence has a verb. This part of a sentence tells us what the subject is doing.

Example

subject → *The man*

verb → *was fishing*

The man was fishing in the creek.

SIMPLE VERBS

Simple verbs are one-word verbs.

Examples

A cat licks its paws.

The teacher spoke to the class.

All the children like pizza.

I lost my hat.

My big tabby cat purrs loudly.

Find the simple verb in each sentence.

1. Jack climbs the ladder.
2. Rosy red apples fell from the tree.
3. Waves crashed onto the sandy beach.
4. The red and white flag flapped in the wind.
5. I bought tickets to a concert at City Hall.

Try this

VERB GROUPS

A **verb group** has more than one word. It is made up of a **helper verb** and other verbs or **participles.** (See Present and past participles pp. 46–47)

A verb group is made up of a 'helper' and other verbs or participles.

Examples

She has eaten all her lunch.

Mum will bake a chocolate cake.

This family is going for a swim at the beach.

I can see you behind that bush!

Mr Griggs has been travelling the world.

Try this

Find the verb group in each sentence.

1. The wind was blowing across the bay.
2. The baby is sleeping in its cot.
3. People have come from everywhere to see the game.
4. I will visit my grandma on Sunday.
5. Tom has been saving his money for a bike.

'HELPER' VERBS (AUXILIARY VERBS)

Helper verbs (also called **auxiliary verbs**) are part of a verb group. They have important jobs to do.

Helper verbs		
am	*is*	*are*
was	*were*	
be	*being*	*been*
do	*does*	*did*
has	*have*	*had*
will	*shall*	

Helper verbs help to:

make **statements**	*They are eating spaghetti.*
ask **questions**	*Have you brought your hat today?*
form **exclamations**	*You should be more careful!*
show **time** (present)	*She is eating jelly beans.*
show **time** (past)	*He was woken by thunder.*
show **time** (future)	*They will go to the beach tomorrow.*
show **voice** (active)	*The dog was eating the bone.*
show **voice** (passive)	*The bone was eaten by the dog.*

Other helpers	
can	*could*
would	*should*
may	*might*
must	

(See Modal verbs p. 51)

The helper verb will always talks about a time in the future.

Some helpers show **ongoing action** in the present time, in the past or in the future. (See Verb tense (present, past and future) pp. 47–50)

Examples

Present	*I am fishing in the river.* *She is waiting for the train.* *They are eating hamburgers.*
Past	*Tom was playing with his Lego blocks.* *The skaters were gliding across the ice.*
Future	*I will see you tomorrow.* *They will be going to the Fun Fair on Saturday.*

Are these events happening in the present, past or future?

1. Jack will take his dog for a walk in the park.
2. We were strolling down a country lane.
3. The acrobats are performing on the high wire.
4. I will be leaving to go to China next week.
5. The cow is chewing her cud.

Try this

A singular subject has a singular verb. A plural subject has a plural verb.

Some **helpers** show whether the verb is **singular** (one) or **plural** (more than one). Remember, a verb must agree with its subject.

(See Subject-verb agreement p. 6)

Examples

I am walking to school.	*They are walking to school.*
She is feeding her pets.	*They are feeding their pets.*
He was reading comics.	*They were reading comics.*
She has woken early.	*They have woken early.*

is and are was and were are very busy helpers!

Add a helper to complete the verb group.

1. I _____ dancing and Erin _____ singing.
2. We _____ painting the gate yellow.
3. They _____ lined up to buy tickets.
4. _____ you bring your hat today?
5. We _____ go to the beach this weekend.

Try this

'BE' VERBS

'Be' verbs are a special set of verbs that link ideas together. 'Be' verbs can be used on their own.

'Be' verbs can work on their own.

'Be' verbs		
am	*is*	*are*
was	*were*	
be	*being*	*been*

Examples

I am nine years old.
Brett was home before dark.
The children are in school.
The horses were in the stable.

'Be' verbs are used to help other verbs and **participles** make a verb group.

A 'be' verb can be a 'helper' in a verb group.

Examples

I am painting the fence.
I will be going to my uncle's farm on Sunday.
Kate has been talking on her mobile phone.
The horses are racing around the track.
The workmen were eating their lunch.

Try this

Find the verb group in each sentence.

1. Mum was hanging the clothes on the line.
2. The farmer's dog is chasing the cattle.
3. The clowns in the circus are juggling balls.
4. We were hurrying to school.
5. Soon, the birds will be flying back to their nests.

'Be' verbs are used to ask **questions**.

Examples

Are you the captain of the hockey team?
Were the answers correct?
Was the train late?
Is she happy now?
Am I allowed to go with you?

'Be' verbs are used with **not** to make a **negative sentence**.

Examples

You are not to feed the wild animals.
Mary is not nine years old yet.
Jake was not ready for school.
I am not tall enough to reach the top shelf.
The children were not in the library.
(See also Contractions p. 53)

positive ***negative***

'HAVE' VERBS

'Have' verbs show ownership or action.
'Have' verbs can be used on their own.

'Have' verbs		
has	*have*	*had*

Examples

Bella has a brand new bike.
Some people have tickets to the Grand Final.
Neva had toast and jam for breakfast.
Jill has a shower before bed.
I have a long walk home.

'Have' verbs are used to help other verbs and **participles** make a verb group.

Examples

Harry has left Brisbane to live in Sydney.
The farmers have planted their wheat crops.
We had walked all the way to school.
Paul has been playing his violin.
The teacher had been watching us play soccer.

Try this

Find the verb group in each sentence.

1. The hikers had taken a wrong turn.
2. Sarah has baked an orange cake.
3. Sophie had made five model planes.
4. They have been planning a holiday to Greece.
5. The cat has eaten all the food in its dish.

'Have' verbs can be used to ask **questions**.

Examples

Has he bought a new bike?
Have you ever been to New Zealand?

'Have' verbs are used with **not** to make a **negative sentence**.

Examples

You have not told me the truth.
Alice has not cleaned her teeth yet.
He had not seen the eagle in its nest.

(See also Contractions p. 53)

'DO' VERBS

'Do' verbs show some action being carried out. 'Do' verbs can be used on their own.

'Do' verbs			
do	does	did	done

Examples

I do my exercises every day.
Bella did her homework.
Mary does her work well.
Jack has done a fine job.

Done is always used with a 'have' verb.

'Do' verbs are most often used to ask **questions**.

Examples

Do you play chess often?
Did you lose your pencil?
Does Jane like fish and chips?

'Do' verbs are used with **not** to make a **negative sentence**.

'Do' verbs with not are often written as contractions: don't, doesn't, didn't.

Examples

I do not know his name.
Meg does not own a red jumper.
They did not hear the school bell.

(See also Contractions p. 53)

PARTICIPLES (PRESENT AND PAST)

(See also Adjectives p. 23)

A **participle** is a word formed from a verb. It is used in a verb group with a **helper**.

Examples

*The baby is **sleeping** in a cot.*
*They are **rowing** across the lake.*
*We were **running** along the beach.*

Helper	Verb	Participle (verb + –ing)
is	sleep	sleeping
are	row	rowing
were	run	running

A verb has two participles — a **present participle** and a **past participle**.
Present participles end in **–ing** *(walking, sitting, eating, playing)*.

They can't have a subject on their own, so they must always have a helper.

Examples

✓ *I am going to the dentist.*	✗ *I going to the dentist.*
✓ *She is cooking a cake.*	✗ *She cooking a cake.*
✓ *The eggs were hatching.*	✗ *The eggs hatching.*

Find the present participle and its helper in each sentence.

1. The surfers are riding the waves.
2. Johnny is singing *Waltzing Matilda*.
3. Sheep were grazing in the green field.
4. I have been waiting here for hours.
5. The sun was shining brightly.

Past participles often end in **-ed** *(washed, puffed, panted, talked).*

They are used in a verb group with a helper. They show past action.

Examples

Dad has watered the garden already.
Alan had waited a long time for the bus.
They have danced before the queen.
A plane has landed on the runway.
The ship was wrecked in the storm.

Some past participles do not end in **-ed**. They have their own special form *(ridden, fallen, kept, sung, written)*. They are used in a verb group with a helper. These are often called **irregular verbs**.

Examples

Jack was bitten by a spider.
They had seen a flock of wild geese.
The sun is hidden by clouds.
Snow had fallen all night long.
I have broken a coffee mug.

VERB TENSE (PRESENT, PAST AND FUTURE)

Verbs say **when** things are happening. **Tense** refers to the point in time they are happening: the present, past or future.

NOW *present tense*	YESTERDAY *past tense*	TOMORROW *future tense*
↓	↓	↓
A man cycles down the hill.	*The man cycled down the hill to the finish line.*	*The man will cycle in a race next Saturday.*

Regular and irregular verbs

Regular verbs have **-s** or **-es**, **-ing**, or **-ed** added to them to show **tense**.

Examples

I ask, he asks, she is asking.
I brush, she brushed, they are brushing.

Complete the table of regular verbs.

I play	I smile	I listen	I clean
He plays	She ________	He ________	She ________
He is playing	She is ________	I am ________	We are ________
They played	We ________	They ________	I ________
We were playing	They were ________	He was ________	She was ________
We have played	She had ________	We have ________	They have ________

Try this

Irregular verbs have their own special **past tense** forms.

Examples

blow	*it blew*	*it was blowing*	*it has blown*
draw	*she drew*	*he was drawing*	*they have drawn*

Complete the table of irregular verbs.

draw	break	know	write
I drew	You broke	She knew	They wrote
I have ________	You have ________	She has ________	They had ________
ride	**sing**	**stand**	**drive**
He rode	They sang	We stood	He drove
He has ________	They had ________	We have ________	He has ________

Present tense

Present tense verbs can be singular or plural.

Here are two ways of showing **present time**:

Add 's' to the verb.

Tense	Number	First person	Second person	Third person
Simple	*Singular*	*I eat apples.*	*You eat apples.*	*He/she/it **eats** apples.*
	Plural	*We eat apples.*	*You eat apples.*	*They eat apples.*
Continuous	*Singular*	*I am eating apples.*	*You are eating apples.*	*He/she/it is eating apples.*
	Plural	*We are eating apples.*	*You are eating apples.*	*They are eating apples.*

For **simple present tense**, add **-s** or **-es** to the verb when it follows a **singular subject** in **third person**.

Examples

I like apples. — *She likes pears.*
I play football. — *He plays cricket.*
I eat mince pies. — *It eats mice and frogs.*
I brush my teeth. — *Sally brushes her hair.*

Past tense

Past tense verbs can be singular or plural.

Here are two ways of showing **past time**:

Tense	Number	First person	Second person	Third person
Simple	*Singular*	*I ran home.*	*You ran home.*	*He/she/it ran home.*
	Plural	*We ran home.*	*You ran home.*	*They ran home.*
Continuous	*Singular*	*I was running.*	*You were running.*	*He/she/it was running.*
	Plural	*We were running.*	*You were running.*	*They were running.*

Future tense

Future tense verbs use the helper **will**.

Examples

I will meet you at the skate park.
They will be going to the football on Saturday.
Will you pay the bus fare?

Story tense

Some stories are told in **present tense** (time).

Stories in present tense contain: am, is, are and many words ending in: –s, –ing

Example

The street is dark and empty.
In a garage, a light shines under the door.
Inside, Sid and his friend, Bee, are working on a machine on the floor of the garage.
The clock on the wall says 2:00 am.
A strong wind rattles the roof.

Try this

Find the verbs that show that the story is written in present tense.

The time machine is shaking. Data is flashing across the computer screen. A cat jumps out and heads for the open door. Sid hits buttons and pulls levers. He looks at the screen and knows that the machine is in countdown…

Most stories are told in **past tense** (time).

Stories in past tense contain: was, were and many verbs ending in: –ed

Example

A gust of wind swirled playfully around Cha. It stirred the dust into a cloud. Cha spread his arms. The wind carried him along. When the wind dropped and the dust settled, Cha was standing at the edge of a wide, green valley. It was covered in thick forest.

Find the verbs that show that the story is written in past tense.

The forest was cool and dim. Vines and creepers snaked through the trees. Soft grasses and ferns covered the forest floor. Cha saw a strange glow in the tree tops. He looked up and saw golden flowers high up in a tree. He grabbed a vine and began to climb. Suddenly, the vine broke and he tumbled to the forest floor.

MODAL VERBS (MODALS)

Modal verbs are **helper verbs** with a special job to do.

Modal verbs	
can	*could*
would	*should*
may	*might*
must	*will*

A modal verb expresses:

possibility — could happen or be done *could, may, might*

obligation — must be done *should, must*

ability — able to be done (or not done) *can, could, can't, couldn't*

permission — allowed to be done (or not done) *can, may, can't, mustn't*

intention — planned to be done *will*

Examples

We could go to the movies if we had money.
You must wash your hands before you eat.
I can run much faster than you.
Mum says we can't go to the beach on our own.
Jake will open his presents soon.

Modal verbs never change their spelling!

You can change statements into questions by starting with a modal verb.

Examples

They can swim.	*You could open the door.*	*I may go home soon.*
Can they swim?	*Could you open the door?*	*May I go home soon?*

Change each statement into a question.

1. Mary will come to the park.
2. I may go mountain climbing.
3. She must do her homework now.
4. We can play cricket tomorrow.
5. You could come with me.

Try this

INFINITIVES

An **infinitive** is made up of two words: **to** plus a **simple verb**.

to + verb = infinitive

Examples

to play	*to learn*	*to buy*
to stand	*to hurry*	*to see*

An important job of the infinitive is to show the **reason** for an action or thought. Infinitives can follow verbs, adjectives, nouns and pronouns.

Examples

I want to go with you.

I am happy to see you again.

Here is a glass of lemonade to drink.

The lifeguard told us to swim between the flags.

Billy is not old enough to go into the surf alone.

An infinitive = to + verb

It answers the question why or what.

Try this

Find the infinitive in each sentence.

1. Dad warned Liam not to play with matches.
2. We are leaving to fly to Japan on Friday.
3. Mum asked you to make your bed.
4. Jessie had nothing left in her lunch box to eat.
5. We expected them to arrive sooner.

CONTRACTIONS

The word **not** makes a sentence negative. It is placed between the **verb** and its helper. The **helper verb** and **not** are often joined together to make one word.

do not ➔ donot ➔ don't

*An **apostrophe** replaces the **letter 'o'** in **'not'**.*

This new word is called a **contraction**. It is most often used in speech.

Examples

I did not see you standing there.

I didn't see you standing there.

She has not eaten her porridge.

She hasn't eaten her porridge.

John does not know how to get there.

John doesn't know how to get there.

Dogs are not allowed on the beach.

Dogs aren't allowed on the beach.

Try this

Match the contractions with the words they replace.

haven't	was not	wouldn't	are not	mustn't	has not
didn't	have not	won't	can not	hasn't	were not
wasn't	could not	aren't	would not	weren't	do not
couldn't	did not	can't	will not	don't	must not

*An **apostrophe** replaces the missing letters.*

A **pronoun subject** and a **helper verb** are often shortened to make one word. This word is also called a **contraction**.

It is written as:
the pronoun + the final one or two letters of the helper verb

she is → she's I will → I'll We have → we've

Try this

What words do the contractions replace in these sentences?

1. You're the only boy in the class with a pet parrot.
2. The sun is going down and it'll soon be dark.
3. He's got five dollars left.
4. They've been for a ride in a hot air balloon.
5. We'd like to buy some jellybeans.

Here is a list of everyday contractions used in speech and informal writing:

I am	*I'm*
I have	*I've*
I had	*I'd*
I would	*I'd*
I will	*I'll*
you are	*you're*
you have	*you've*
you had	*you'd*
you would	*you'd*
you will	*you'll*
it is	*it's*
it has	*it's*
it would	*it'd*
it had	*it'd*
it will	*it'll*
that is	*that's*
that has	*that's*
that will	*that'll*
that had	*that'd*
that would	*that'd*

she is	*she's*
she has	*she's*
she had	*she'd*
she would	*she'd*
she will	*she'll*
we are	*we're*
we have	*we've*
we had	*we'd*
we would	*we'd*
we will	*we'll*
let us	*let's*
could have	*could've*
should have	*should've*
would have	*would've*
here is	*here's*
there is	*there's*
there has	*there's*
there had	*there'd*
there would	*there'd*
there will	*there'll*

he is	*he's*
he has	*he's*
he had	*he'd*
he would	*he'd*
she will	*she'll*
they are	*they're*
they have	*they've*
they had	*they'd*
they would	*they'd*
they will	*they'll*
where is	*where's*
when is	*when's*
what is	*what's*
why is	*why's*
what has	*what's*
who is	*who's*
who has	*who's*
who have	*who've*
who would	*who'd*
who will	*who'll*

VOICE

Voice refers to the kinds of verbs used — **active verbs** or **passive verbs**.
A verb is **active** when the **subject is doing the action**.
A verb is **passive** when the **subject is being acted upon**.

Examples

Active	Passive
The dog chased the fox.	*The fox was chased by the dog.*
The boy threw the ball.	*The ball was thrown by the boy.*
Kim scored the first goal.	*The first goal was scored by Kim.*
Storms lashed the coast.	*The coast was lashed by storms.*

VERB WRAP-UP

Types of verbs	Doing (action), saying, thinking, feeling, 'be', 'do' and 'have' verbs.
Simple verbs	One-word verbs. *(spin, sleep, kick, bite, cook)*
Verb group	Group of words that function as a verb. *(is going, has been hidden)*
Helper (auxiliary) verbs	Verbs that help other verbs in a verb group. *(The ball **is bouncing**.)* Some helper verbs can work on their own. *(The ball **is** round.)*
Present participles	Verbs ending in **–ing**. *(snowing, reading, walking, riding)*
Past participles	Verbs ending in **–ed**. *(cooked, danced, bubbled)* Some have their own special form. *(hidden, kept, written)* Often called irregular verbs.
Tense	Verbs say **when** things happen: **Present** — *I talk, he talks, we are talking* **Past** — *I talked, he was talking, we were talking* **Future** — *I will talk, he will talk, they will talk*
Regular verbs	Add **–s**, **–ing** and **–ed** to show tense. *(she talk**s**, he is talk**ing**, we talk**ed**)*
Irregular verbs	Have their own special past tense and past participle forms. *(**grow:** he grew, he has grown; **sing:** she sang, she has sung)*
Subject-verb agreement	A **singular subject** has a **singular verb**. *(The **girl is** dancing.)* A **plural subject** has a **plural verb**. *(The **girls are** dancing.)*
Modal verbs	Helpers that change verb meanings. *(I **might** come. You **must** go now.)*
Infinitives	**to + verb** *(to shout, to read, to stand)*
Contractions	Phrases shortened to one word: **helper verb + not** *(haven't, isn't, didn't)* **pronoun + helper verb** *(it's, we've, they're)*
Voice	**Active:** The subject does the action. *(The dog bit the boy.)* **Passive:** The subject receives the action. *(The boy was bitten by the dog.)*

ADVERBS

Adverbs add meaning to verbs. They add extra information about what people and things are doing.

Adverbs add meaning and extra information to verbs.

They say:

HOW things are being done *(manner)*

WHEN things are happening *(time)*

WHERE things are happening *(place)*.

ADVERBS OF MANNER

Adverbs of manner show **how** something is being done. Many adverbs of manner end in **–ly** and are built from adjectives.

Examples

strong **+ *ly***	*loud* **+ *ly***	*silent* **+ *ly***	*late* **+ *ly***
strongly	***loudly***	***silently***	***lately***

When an adjective ends in –y, change the –y to –i before adding –ly.

Adverbs of manner say more about the verb.

Examples

Byron swam strongly back to shore.
*(**How** did Byron swim?)*

*Tom ran home quickly. (**How** did Tom run?)*

Mum gently rocked the baby to sleep.
*(**How** did Mum rock the baby?)*

Try this

Find the adverbs and the verbs that they add meaning to.

1. Kay sat quietly at her desk.
2. Stack the books neatly on the shelf.
3. It rained heavily all night.
4. The children are chatting loudly.
5. Cut around the picture carefully.

Create a list of adverbs by adding –ly to these adjectives.

1. clear
2. angry
3. excited
4. lazy
5. foolish
6. tidy
7. tired
8. soft
9. steady
10. wild

ADVERBS OF TIME

Adverbs of time say **when** things are happening. They can be single words or phrases. (See Adverb phrases p. 65)

Examples

yesterday *long ago* *now*
tomorrow *on Tuesday*

Adverbs of time also tell **how often** things happen.

Examples

sometimes *often* *twice* *weekly*

Adverbs of time say more about the verb.

Adverbs of time can show sequence: firstly..., secondly..., finally...

Examples

We will meet you at the park later.
*(**When** will we meet?)*

Millie won her race today.
*(**When** did Millie win?)*

I go to football training weekly.
*(**How often** do I go?)*

Find the adverbs and the verbs they add meaning to.

1. We often go bushwalking in the mountains.
2. I think that it will rain soon.
3. You go now and I'll come later.
4. Yesterday, I found a dollar on the footpath.
5. Sometimes I bake biscuits for my family.

Try this

Here is a list of adverbs of time that people often use:

early	*yesterday*	*daily*	*sometimes*	*always*
late	*tomorrow*	*weekly*	*often*	*never*
afterwards	*next*	*usually*	*seldom*	*then*

ADVERBS OF PLACE

Adverbs of place say **where** things are happening. They can be single words or phrases. (See Adverb phrases p. 65)

Adverbs of place say where things happen.

Examples

here there anywhere behind

Adverbs of place say more about the verb.

Examples

*The birds flew away. (**Where** did the birds fly?)*

I will hide myself somewhere.
*(**Where** will I hide?)*

They ran off and left me behind.
*(**Where** did they leave me?)*

Find the adverbs and the verbs they add meaning to.

1. There it is!
2. The plane is flying high.
3. Here is the sock I lost.
4. Danny has gone outside.
5. I came first in the race.

Try this

NEGATIVE ADVERBS

The **adverbs not** and **never** are called **negative adverbs** because they are used to make a sentence negative. Negative adverbs often appear as a **contraction**. (See Contractions p. 53)

Not and never are negative adverbs.

Yes is positive.

Examples

You are not to go to the park by yourself.
Suzie is never on time.
I don't have any money.

Make these sentences negative.

1. She can make pancakes.
2. Jackson was able to climb the apple tree.
3. I hope I see you again.
4. Your answers are correct.
5. We could go fishing in the creek.

Try this

INTERROGATIVE ADVERBS (QUESTION)

Some adverbs can be used to ask **questions**. They are called **interrogative adverbs**.

Examples

How old are you?	*How tall are you?*
When is your birthday?	*When will you be nine?*
Where do you live?	*Where do you go to school?*
Why are you crying?	*Why is the dog barking?*

Interrogative adverbs ask questions: How? When? Where? Why?

Try this

Use an adverb to ask each question.

1. ______ many children are in your class?
2. ______ will you return from your holiday?
3. ______ did you go on Sunday?
4. ______ were you late for school?
5. ______ often do you play your violin?

MODAL ADVERBS

Some adverbs can be placed before an adjective or another adverb. They are called **modal adverbs**.

Their job is to:

1. **modify** the meaning *(change it a little bit)*

Examples

almost ripe *rather late* *fairly soon*

2. **intensify** the meaning *(make it stronger)*.

absolutely certain *very tired* *extremely far*

Here is a list of modal adverbs used with **adjectives**: **adverb + adjective.**

really happy	*deeply sad*	*very popular*	*quite old*
entirely wrong	*fairly comfortable*	*completely satisfied*	*extremely rich*

Here is a list of modal adverbs used with **adverbs**: **adverb + adverb.**

too loudly	*somewhat early*	*very fast*	*quite sure*
almost there	*nearly there*	*shortly afterwards*	*never again*

ADVERB WRAP-UP

Adverbs	Words that say more about a verb, an adjective or other adverb.
Types of adverbs	Adverbs of manner, time and place; negative adverbs, interrogative adverbs, modal adverbs.
Adverbs of manner	Say **how** things happen. *(He runs **quickly**. The wind blew **strongly**.)*
Adverbs of time	Say **when** things happen. *(Come here **now**. I'll come **tomorrow**.)* Say **how often** things happen. *(**Sometimes** we play chess.)*
Adverbs of place	Say **where** things happen. *(**Here** is your hat! Don't leave it **behind**.)*
Negative adverbs	Use **not** and **never** to make a sentence negative. *(They **never** saw the fox again. He is **not** ready for school yet. I **can't** play netball.)*
Interrogative adverbs	Introduce **questions**. *(**When** is your birthday? **How** old are you? **Where** do you live? **Why** are you crying?)*
Modal adverbs	**Modify** meaning. *(He's **quite** tall. The apple is **almost** ripe.)* **Intensify** meaning. *(I'm **very** happy. I'm **really** worried.)*

PHRASES

A phrase is a group of words that go together.

A phrase is a 'chunk' or group of words that go together. They do not make sense on their own because they do not have a verb.

Examples

down the hill	*over the bridge*
across the sea	*to New Zealand*

A phrase is always part of a **sentence**.

Examples

Tilly rode her bike down the hill and over the bridge.

Last week, the ship sailed across the sea to New Zealand.

A ball rolled through the gate and into the gutter.

A phrase adds valuable information to a sentence.

A phrase is often used to answer a **question**.

Examples

Where *are you going? Over to Tim's.*

When are you going on holiday? On Saturday.

Where is my hat? Over here on the table.

A phrase can begin with a **preposition** or a **participle**.

PREPOSITION PHRASES

A **preposition phrase** begins with a **preposition**. The preposition comes before a **noun** (or **pronoun**) and connects it to the other ideas in the sentence.

Examples

to, from	*William took an orange from Kate and gave it to Fred.*
over, under	*I climbed over the fence, but my dog went under it.*
to, on, by	*Ken goes to school on his bike, but I go by car.*

Here is a short list of prepositions used to introduce phrases.

at	*by*	*down*	*of*	*since*	*up*
about	*before*	*for*	*off*	*to*	*upon*
above	*beside*	*from*	*on*	*towards*	*under*
across	*behind*	*into*	*over*	*through*	*with*
after	*below*	*near*	*past*	*until*	*without*

ADJECTIVE PHRASES

Some phrases do the work of an **adjective**. They must follow the **noun** they describe. Many **adjective phrases** begin with a **preposition**.

An adjective phrase says more about a noun.

Examples

a ***cup*** *of tea*
a ***vase*** *of flowers*
a ***packet*** *of chips*
a ***box*** *of chocolates*
the ***captain*** *of the team*
a ***bird*** *in a cage*
a ***boy*** *in Year 3*
a ***girl*** *with red hair*
a ***man*** *in uniform*
the ***person*** *in charge*

Find the adjective phrase. Which noun does it describe?

1. Mr Budd bought a shirt with blue stripes.
2. He gave his mum a big bunch of roses.
3. The tree beside the gate is loaded with apples.
4. I'll have the cake with chocolate icing, thanks.
5. A girl in a pink dress is standing at the bus stop.

Try this

TROUBLESPOT

An adjective phrase must always follow the noun it describes.

✔ A lady in a red dress is playing the piano.
✘ A lady is playing the piano in a red dress.

✔ A man in uniform drove the army truck.
✘ A man drove the army truck in uniform.

✔ He put the bird with a broken wing into a box.
✘ He put the bird into a box with a broken wing.

PARTICIPLE PHRASES

Participle phrases do the work of adjectives.

A **participle phrase** can begin with a **present participle**.

The phrase does the work of an **adjective**.
(See Participles (present and past) p. 23)

Examples

*I saw a **boy** eating ice cream.*

*Standing on tip-toe, **Kelly** could see over the fence.*

*None of the **people** waiting for the bus had umbrellas.*

*Running down the lane, **Graham** tripped and fell.*

*That **boy** riding down the hill is going too fast.*

A **participle phrase** can begin with a **past participle**.

The phrase does the work of an **adjective**.
(See Participles (present and past) p. 23)

Examples

*A **truck** loaded with coal arrived at the port.*

*I like **toast** spread with honey.*

*We listened to a **song** sung by the school choir.*

*We live in a stone **cottage** built a hundred years ago.*

*She handed me a **note** written on blue paper.*

Try this

Find the participle phrase. Which noun does it describe?

1. A boy dressed in striped pyjamas ran down the stairs.
2. Standing on his chair, Nick could see out the window.
3. I love chocolates filled with creamy caramel.
4. Wearing swimming costumes, the children ran to the beach.
5. Ellen skipped around the room holding her teddy bear.

ADVERB PHRASES

Some phrases do the work of an **adverb**. They usually say more about the **verb** by saying **how**, **when** and **where** things are happening. They are called **adverb phrases**.

Adverb phrases say how, when and where things happen.

PHRASES

Examples

How/How Long	*When*	*Where*
for an hour	*after dark*	*in the garden*
with a big smile	*in the morning*	*above the clouds*
faster and faster	*tomorrow afternoon*	*across the street*
like a baby	*in a minute*	*under the sea*
in a soft voice	*before the test*	*over there*
for a week	*on Sunday*	*on the bed*

Adverb phrases often begin with **prepositions**.

Examples

With a big smile, Greg opened his gift. ***(how)***

We had to wait for an hour to catch the train. ***(how long)***

I am going to the movies on Friday. ***(when)***

They are strolling along the beach. ***(where)***

Add an adverb phrase.

1. The bus will leave *(when?)* **at** ________________________.
2. Tomorrow, we are driving *(where?)* **to** ________________________.
3. Bake in a hot oven *(how long?)* **for** ________________________.
4. The boys walked *(where?)* **across** ________________________.
5. He growled *(how?)* **like** ________________________.

Try this

PHRASE WRAP-UP

Phrase	A group of words that is part of a sentence. It has no verb.
Preposition phrases	Phrases beginning with a **preposition**. *(**to** the door, **on** the table, **under** the chair, **over** the hill)*
Adjective phrases	Phrases doing the work of adjectives. Adjective phrases **must** follow the nouns they describe. *(a man **in a truck**, the jug **on the table**, a box **of toys**)*
Participle phrases	Phrases beginning with participles that do the work of adjectives. **Present participle:** *a lady **wearing a sunhat**, the boy **eating plums*** **Past participle:** *a car **covered in dust**, the ball **hidden in the grass***
Adverb phrases	Phrases doing the work of adverbs. They say **how**, **how long**, **when** and **where** things happen. *(Cook **for two minutes**. He ran **up the hill**. She spoke **in a whisper**. See you **in the morning**.)*

PUNCTUATION

Punctuation is used to help readers make meaning.

Punctuation is a marking system that writers use to help readers make meaning. It clearly marks where each **sentence** begins and ends. Punctuation separates words inside a sentence, so the reader does not run every word together and lose track of the meaning.

STATEMENTS

Statements begin with **capital letters** and end with **full stops**.

Example

Meerkats are small mammals. They live in South Africa. They dig tunnels underground to live in and stay cool in the hot desert sun. Meerkats live in large groups called mobs. They eat mostly insects. One meerkat usually acts as a lookout. It stands up tall and watches out for enemies.

COMMANDS

Commands begin with **capital letters** and end with **full stops (.)**.

Examples

1. *Put the butter and sugar in a bowl.*
2. *Beat until soft and creamy.*
3. *Add two eggs.*
4. *Pour in one cup of milk.*

QUESTIONS

Questions begin with **capital letters** and end with **question marks (?)**.

Examples

Have you been to Townsville?
Do you like green jelly?
Are there any apples left?

EXCLAMATIONS

Exclamations begin with **capital letters** and end with **exclamation marks (!)**.

Examples

I don't believe it!

Go away!

What! Late again!

Use the correct punctuation marker at the end of each sentence.

1. A parrot is a bird with colourful feathers
2. Have you the seen the dinosaurs at the museum
3. Did you have bacon and eggs for breakfast
4. You must never, ever do that again
5. Tim goes to football training on Friday nights

Try this

CAPITAL LETTERS

Capital letters mark the first word in a sentence. They also name people, places and events. These words are called **proper nouns**.

(See Proper nouns p. 15)

Examples

John and Betty May live in Applegate Street in the suburb of Sunnyhills in Brisbane.

We sailed under the Sydney Harbour Bridge and visited the Opera House.

Athletes from India arrived on Saturday to compete in the Olympic Games.

Capital letters also mark the first **spoken word** in a conversation.

Examples

Mary asked, "What time does the game start?"

Jim replied, "It starts at three o'clock."

"Come on," said Ben. "Let's play cricket."

"Okay," said Jack. "You can bat first."

Which words should begin with a capital letter?

1. jack ross is a jockey. last year, he rode the horse, dark storm, in australia's famous race, the melbourne cup.
2. my brother, joshua, will fly to italy in august to study art at a school in rome.
3. katy said, "let's have a game of monopoly, mark." mark smiled. "okay," he said. "let's ask rosie to play too."

Try this

COMMAS

Commas (,) are used to show the reader where to make a small break between words. They mark off words that 'go together', which helps the reader read fluently and with understanding.

Example

Kangaroos are native animals of Australia. They have strong back legs, short front legs and a long tail. They are the largest marsupials in the world, standing over two metres tall. They eat grass, shrubs and tree leaves.

Commas separate words in a **list**.

Examples

I like apples, pears, plums and grapes. Terry prefers oranges, peaches, bananas and figs.

You will need eggs, milk, sugar and flour to make pancakes.

Try this

Where should commas be placed in these sentences?

1. Jenkins is a tall dark handsome young man.
2. We packed our gear for camp: a tent cooking pots sleeping bags and food.
3. Mum bought eggs cheese milk a cabbage and some potatoes.
4. We saw elephants tigers lions and zebras at the zoo.
5. Ellie Anne Susan and Karen walk home together after school.

Commas mark off an **adverb** or **phrase** at the **beginning of a sentence**.

Examples

Suddenly, everything went quiet and no-one spoke.

Later that day, we went for a swim. Afterwards, we went for a walk on the beach.

By day, the meerkats bathe in the sun and scavenge for food. At night, they go back to their underground tunnels.

Try this

Where should commas be placed in these sentences?

1. Last weekend Dad painted the gutters dark green.
2. Carefully John made his way down the mountain side.
3. During that long evening wind and rain lashed the coast.
4. Without thinking Ken grabbed his bike and chased the robber.
5. Finally top the pizza with grated cheese.

Commas mark off a phrase in the **middle of a sentence**.

If you left out the phrase, the sentence would still make sense.

Examples

This story, like many others, is about fairies and elves.

Sorry, my friend, I can't come with you today.

Lightning flashed and, within a few minutes, the storm struck.

Try this

Where should commas be placed in these sentences?

1. Harry his face white whispered something in my ear.
2. My model plane landed upside down in a ditch.
3. Ashley her face shining opened her birthday gift.
4. The dog was sitting there outside the shop waiting for its master.
5. The string broke and within seconds my kite disappeared.

Commas divide a sentence into **groups of ideas**. Without commas, the ideas would not be clearly marked. The sentence would be a jumble of ideas and difficult to understand.

Read this sentence aloud, with and without commas, to see which one is easier to read and makes better sense.

1. The hiker who had been lost for many days was found sheltering in a large dark dry cave.
2. The hiker, who had been lost for many days, was found sheltering in a large, dark, dry cave.

If a comma is left out of a sentence it can greatly change the meaning of the sentence.

Examples

"I like cooking Mum," said Sally.
"I like cooking, Mum," said Sally.

When Bill had eaten his dog came running to the back door.
When Bill had eaten, his dog came running to the back door.

While I was cleaning my sister made a cup of tea.
While I was cleaning, my sister made a cup of tea.

Try this

Where should commas be placed in these sentences?

1. "Let's eat Grandpa," said Joe.
2. When the storm broke Jake took cover in the shed
3. While I was cooking Brad set the table.
4. Melbourne on the banks of the Yarra River is a busy bustling city.
5. After my family moved the house was sold.

SPEECH MARKS

Speech marks (" ") are used to show **spoken words** in a conversation.
A **comma** marks off the spoken words from the rest of the sentence.

Example

"Dinner is on the table," called Mum.
"Thanks, I'm coming," said Jess.
"Me too!" said Jy.

Punctuate these conversations.

1. Where did you go for your holiday Sam? asked Dennis.
Dennis replied I went to the beach with my family.
2. The teacher said put your homework books on my table please.
Barry stood up and mumbled sir I left my homework at home.
3. Here's five dollars Ava said Mum. Go to the shop and buy some milk, please.
Sure mum said Ava. May I buy a Freddo too?

Try this

APOSTROPHES

An **apostrophe (')** is used to show ownership.
For a single owner, add **'s**.
For more than one owner, place the apostrophe after the owners: **s'**. (See Possessive nouns pp. 15–16)

Examples

There are balls, bears and battleships in Gerry's toy box.

I saw Pepper's name on the dog's collar.

The teacher marked Kate's homework and Gary's artwork.

Several birds' nests were blown apart in the storm.

The boys' coats are hanging in the cupboard.

For **irregular plural** owners, add **'s** after the owners.

Examples

The children's socks are hanging on the line.
Dad bought a new tie at the men's store.
We saw mice's paw prints in the spilt sugar.

Place the apostrophes correctly.

1. A cats fur is soft and silky.
2. We saw boys footprints in the sand.
3. I fed my sisters budgie and my dads snake.
4. Spiders webs hung from every branch.
5. The childrens books are on the teachers table.

An apostrophe is also used to mark a **contraction**. (See Contractions p. 53)

Examples

I don't like tomato soup.
She isn't home yet.
The hen hasn't laid any eggs.
The horses aren't in the stable.
It's a long way to the beach.
She's feeling tired so she'll go to bed.
He's seven and I'm eight.
I've seen what you're doing.

Apostrophes mark missing letters in contractions.

Place the apostrophes correctly.

1. The fishermen havent caught any fish yet.
2. Wheres Tom going?
3. Its too far to walk, so well take the bus.
4. He didnt have any money, so he couldnt buy an ice cream.
5. Lets hide so Kelly cant find us.

PUNCTUATION WRAP-UP

Full stops	Markers placed at the end of statements. (*The baby is in her cot*.) Markers placed at the end of commands. (*Boil the egg for two minutes*.)
Question marks	Markers placed at the end of questions. (*Do you like mangoes***?**)
Exclamation marks	Markers placed at the end of exclamations. (*I can't believe you've lost your hat***!** *How silly***!**)
Capital letters	Mark the **first word** in a sentence. (***A** butterfly is a beautiful insect.*) Mark **proper nouns.** *(We will visit **B**rian in **P**erth in **J**une or **J**uly.)* Mark the first **spoken word**. *(Mum asked, "**W**here is he?" Sam replied, "**H**e's at the skate park.")*
Commas	Separate words in a **list.** (*He grows apples***,** *plums***,** *peaches and pears.*) Mark off an **adverb** or **phrase** at the **beginning of a sentence.** (*Suddenly***,** *the trail disappeared. After five minutes***,** *he knew he was lost.*) Mark off a **phrase** in the **middle of a sentence.** (*Jackson stood quietly***,** *hands on hips***,** *waiting for the door to open.)* Mark off **spoken words** from the rest of the sentence. (*The teacher asked***,** *"Why are you late?" "My bike had a flat tyre***,***" answered Bill.*)
Speech marks	Mark the **spoken words** of a speaker. *(**"**I am as tall as you,**"** said Patrick.)*
Apostrophes	Mark a noun to show **ownership**. (*Jack's bike, the teacher's name; men's golf clubs, children's toys; birds' nests, foxes' red eyes*) Mark letters missing in a **contraction**. (*didn't, wasn't, haven't, isn't; they're, it's, we've, she's, you'll*)

Try this

ANSWERS

Page

1 Sentences

We went for a ride on the merry-go-round at the Royal Show.
Ash from the volcano fell on the village.
It looks like rain, so you will need to take an umbrella.

2 Statements

1. Opinion
2. Fact
3. Opinion
4. Fact
5. Fact

6 Subject and object

1. Mum *(subject)* put **a bowl of soup** *(object)* in front of me.
2. Ben and his friends are playing **chess** in the library.
3. The female magpie builds **her nest** high up in the fork of a tree.
4. Every morning and afternoon, the farmer milks **the cows**.
5. Jan baked **a chocolate cake** for afternoon tea.

7 Simple sentences

1. The sun is shining brightly today.
2. Would you like an orange?
3. Before school, I feed my pet fish.
4. A big, silver plane landed on the runway.
5. There, at the door, stood my best friend.

8 Compound sentences

1. Would you like an orange or would you like an apple? (Would you like an orange or an apple?)
2. I would like to buy this hat, but it costs too much.
3. You make the toast and I'll cook the eggs.
4. It rained last night, so the grass is very wet.
5. Harry went to the gym and William went with him.

Page

12 Compound nouns

1. thunderstorm, weekend
2. softball, netball
3. milkshake, popcorn
4. toothpaste, toothbrush,
5. farmyard, horseback

13 Number (plural nouns)

bones, pigs, brushes, kisses
foxes, horses, baskets, beaches
trumpets, games, teachers, oranges
gases, bunches, carrots, boxes

14 Irregular nouns

gullies, kites, matches, loaves
trains, footpaths, women, shoes
elves, geese, halves, keys

15 Proper nouns

1. *Waltzing Matilda*, Australia Day
2. March, Bob, Snowy Mountains
3. Mr Brown, Cairns, Holden
4. Mrs Smith, Woolworths, Friday
5. David Morris, Winter Olympics, Sochi

16 Possessive nouns

1. Mum's *(singular)*, Dad's *(singular)*
2. rabbits' *(plural)*
3. spiders' *(plural)*, sun's *(singular)*
4. athletes' *(plural)*
5. magpies' *(plural)*

17 Gender nouns

Male: rooster, uncle, father, prince
Female: princess, grandma, lady, mare
Male or female: driver, hero, foal, baby
Neither male nor female: planet, wheat, car, book

18 Noun groups

1. a strong wind; the grey clouds
2. two red tomatoes; some cheese
3. an exciting football game
4. heavy rain
5. one man; a silver trumpet

Page

22 Adjectives: Describing

1. A **large** *(adjective)* parcel *(noun)* came in the mail.
2. Ken has **dark brown** eyes.
3. After a **few** months, Sally had **enough** money to buy **new** shoes.
4. The **golden** coach was pulled by **six white** horses.
5. Dan was the **first** person to cross the **finishing** line.

22 Adjective phrases

1. The clothes *(noun)* **on the line** *(adjective phrase)* are nearly dry.
2. A boy **with a note** came to the door of our classroom.
3. He looked closely at the photo **on the wall**.
4. You will need to bring a box **of spare batteries**.
5. The sheep **in the top paddock** will soon be shorn.

23 Participles (present and past): Verbal adjectives

1. I am wearing my new **swimming** costume.
2. I like **steamed** vegetables and **baked** potatoes.
3. He carried a **lighted** candle.
4. There was a **surprised** look on his face.
5. A man is fishing in the **flowing** river.

25 Adjective suffixes: Antonyms

1. hopeful, hopeless
2. careful, careless
3. thoughtful, thoughtless
4. restful, restless
5. helpful, helpless

26 Adjectives of degree: Suffixes

1. youngest
2. faster
3. older
4. sweetest
5. shorter

26 Adjectives of degree: More or most

1. more
2. most
3. more
4. most
5. most

Page

31 Person

1. first person
2. second person
3. first person
4. third person
5. third person

33 Possessive pronouns

1. his
2. hers
3. their
4. your
5. mine

34 Reflexive pronouns

1. myself
2. himself
3. yourself
4. herself
5. themselves

34 Interrogative pronouns

1. What
2. Whose
3. Which
4. Who
5. What

35 Indefinite pronouns

1. anyone (anybody)
2. no-one (nobody)
3. Everyone (Everybody)
4. something
5. someone (somebody, anyone, anybody)

37 Pronoun reference

1. **her, she** — Gemma; **its** — teddy bear
2. **his** — Jarrod; **they** — Jarrod and his brother; **them** — toys
3. **you, your** — David
4. **you, him** — Gerry; **my** — Joe
5. **our, us** — Stan and I; **they** — friends; **them** — lollies

39 Simple verbs

1. climbs
2. fell
3. crashed
4. flapped
5. bought

Page

40 Verb groups

1. was blowing
2. is sleeping
3. have come
4. will visit
5. has been saving

41 Helper verbs (auxiliary verbs): Time

1. future
2. past
3. present
4. future
5. present

42 Helper verbs (auxiliary verbs): Singular and plural

1. am, is (was, was)
2. are (were)
3. are (were)
4. Did
5. will

43 'Be' verbs

1. was hanging
2. is chasing
3. are juggling
4. were hurrying
5. will be flying

44 'Have' verbs

1. had taken
2. has baked
3. had made
4. have been planning
5. has eaten

46 Participles (present + helper)

1. are riding
2. is singing
3. were grazing
4. have been waiting
5. was shining

Page

48 Verb tense: Regular verbs

I smile	I listen	I clean
She smiles	He listens	She cleans
She is smiling	I am listening	We are cleaning
We smiled	They listened	I cleaned
They were smiling	He was listening	She was cleaning
She had smiled	We have listened	They have cleaned

48 Verb tense: Irregular verbs

draw	break	know	write
I drew	You broke	She knew	They wrote
I have drawn	You have broken	She has known	They had written
ride	**sing**	**stand**	**drive**
He rode	They sang	We stood	He drove
He has ridden	They had sung	We have stood	He has driven

50 Story tense: Present tense

The time machine **is shaking**. Data **is flashing** across the computer screen. A cat **jumps out** and **heads** for the open door. Sid **hits** buttons and **pulls** levers. He **looks** at the screen and **knows** that the machine **is** in countdown...

50 Story tense: Past tense

The forest **was** cool and dim. Vines and creepers **snaked** through the trees. Soft grasses and ferns **covered** the forest floor. Cha **saw** a strange glow in the tree tops. He **looked up** and **saw** golden flowers high up in a tree. He **grabbed** a vine and **began** to climb. Suddenly, the vine **broke** and he **tumbled** to the forest floor.

51 Modal verbs

1. Will Mary come to the park?
2. May I go mountain climbing?
3. Must she do her homework now?
4. Can we play cricket tomorrow?
5. Could you come with me?

Page

52 Infinitives

1. to play
2. to fly
3. to make
4. to eat
5. to arrive

53 Contractions

haven't	have not
didn't	did not
wasn't	was not
couldn't	could not

wouldn't	would not
won't	will not
aren't	are not
can't	can not

mustn't	must not
hasn't	has not
weren't	were not
don't	do not

54 Contractions

1. You're — You are
2. it'll — it will
3. He's — He has
4. They've — They have
5. We'd — We would

57 Adverbs of manner

1. Kay sat *(verb)* **quietly** *(adverb)* at her desk.
2. Stack the books **neatly** on the shelf.
3. It rained **heavily** all night.
4. The children are chatting **loudly**.
5. Cut around the picture **carefully**.

57 Adverbs of manner

1. clearly
2. angrily
3. excitedly
4. lazily
5. foolishly
6. tidily
7. tiredly
8. softly
9. steadily
10. wildly

58 Adverbs of time

1. We **often** *(adverb)* go bushwalking *(verb)* in the mountains.
2. I think that it will rain **soon**.
3. You go **now** and I'll come **later**.
4. **Yesterday**, I found a dollar on the footpath.
5. **Sometimes** I bake biscuits for my family.

Page

59 Adverbs of place

1. **There** *(adverb)* it is *(verb)*!
2. The plane is flying **high**.
3. **Here** is the sock I lost.
4. Danny has gone **outside**.
5. I came **first** in the race.

59 Negative adverbs

1. She can**not** make pancakes.
   She can **never** make pancakes.
2. Jackson was **not** able to climb the apple tree.
   Jackson was **never** able to climb the apple tree.
3. I hope I **never** see you again.
4. Your answers are **not** correct.
   Your answers are **never** correct.
5. We could **not** go fishing in the creek.
   We could **never** go fishing in the creek.

60 Interrogative adverbs

1. How
2. When
3. Where
4. Why
5. How

63 Adjective phrases

1. Mr Budd bought a shirt *(noun)* **with blue stripes** *(adjective phrase)*.
2. He gave his mum a big bunch **of roses**.
3. The tree **beside the gate** is loaded with apples.
4. I'll have the cake **with chocolate icing**, thanks.
5. A girl **in a pink dress** is standing at the bus stop.

64 Participle phrases

1. A boy *(noun)* **dressed in striped pyjamas** *(participle phrase)* ran down the stairs.
2. **Standing on his chair**, Nick could see out the window.
3. I love chocolates **filled with creamy caramel**.
4. **Wearing swimming costumes**, the children ran to the beach.
5. Ellen skipped around the room **holding her teddy bear**.

65 Adverb phrases

Answers will vary.

Page

68 Punctuation

1. A parrot is a bird with colourful feathers.
2. Have you the seen the dinosaurs at the museum**?**
3. Did you have bacon and eggs for breakfast**?**
4. You must never, ever do that again**!**
5. Tim goes to football training on Friday nights.

69 Capital letters

1. **Jack Ross** is a jockey. **Last** year, he rode the horse, **Dark Storm**, in **Australia's** famous race, the **Melbourne Cup**.
2. **My** brother, **Joshua**, will fly to **Italy** in **August** to study art at a school in **Rome**.
3. **Katy** said, "**Let's** have a game of **Monopoly**, **Mark**."
   Mark smiled. "**Okay**," he said. "**Let's** ask **Rosie** to play too."

69 Commas: List

1. Jenkins is a tall**,** dark and handsome young man.
2. We packed our gear for camp: a tent**,** cooking pots**,** sleeping bags and food.
3. Mum bought eggs**,** cheese**,** milk**,** a cabbage and some potatoes.
4. We saw elephants**,** tigers**,** lions and zebras at the zoo.
5. Ellie**,** Anne**,** Susan and Karen walk home together after school.

70 Commas: Beginning of a sentence

1. Last weekend**,** Dad painted the gutters dark green.
2. Carefully**,** John made his way down the mountain side.
3. During that long evening**,** wind and rain lashed the coast.
4. Without thinking**,** Ken grabbed his bike and chased the robber.
5. Finally**,** top the pizza with grated cheese.

70 Commas: Middle of a sentence

1. Harry**,** his face white**,** whispered something in my ear.
2. My model plane landed**,** upside down**,** in a ditch.
3. Ashley**,** her face shining**,** opened her birthday gift.

Page

4. The dog was sitting there**,** outside the shop**,** waiting for its master.
5. The string broke and**,** within seconds**,** my kite disappeared.

71 Commas: Oral exercise

The hiker, who had been lost for many days, was found sheltering in a large, dark, dry cave.

71 Commas: Placement of commas

1. "Let's eat**,** Grandpa**,**" said Joe.
2. When the storm broke**,** Jake took cover in the shed
3. While I was cooking**,** Brad set the table.
4. Melbourne**,** on the banks of the Yarra River**,** is a busy**,** bustling city.
5. After my family moved**,** the house was sold.

72 Speech marks

1. **"**Where did you go for your holiday, Sam?**"** asked Dennis.
   Dennis replied, **"**I went to the beach with my family.**"**
2. The teacher said, **"P**ut your homework books on my table, please.**"**
   Barry stood up and mumbled, **"S**ir, I left my homework at home.**"**
3. **"**Here's five dollars, Ava,**"** said Mum. **"**Go to the shop and buy some milk, please.**"**
   "Sure **M**um,**"** said Ava. **"**May I buy a Freddo too?**"**

73 Apostrophes: Ownership

1. A cat**'**s fur is soft and silky.
2. We saw boys**'** footprints in the sand.
3. I fed my sister**'**s budgie and my dad**'**s snake.
4. Spiders**'** webs hung from every branch.
5. The children**'**s books are on the teacher**'**s table.

73 Apostrophes: Contractions

1. The fishermen haven**'**t caught any fish yet.
2. Where**'**s Tom going?
3. It**'**s too far to walk, so we**'**ll take the bus.
4. He didn**'**t have any money, so he couldn**'**t buy an ice cream.
5. Let**'**s hide so Kelly can**'**t find us.

GLOSSARY

active verb	A **verb** that shows the subject doing the action. *The dog* ***chased*** *the fox. The boy* ***threw*** *the ball.*
active voice	Voice refers to the kinds of verbs used. The **verb** (and voice) is active when the subject is doing the action. *The cat* ***chased*** *the mouse.*
adjective	A word that describes a person, place or thing. *an* ***old*** *bag, a* ***red*** *car,* ***hot*** *potatoes,* ***strong*** *wind*
adjective phrase	A group of words that says more about the noun it follows. *A clown* ***in baggy trousers****. A cat* ***with long whiskers****.*
adjective suffix	An ending added to a word to make it an adjective. *help****ful****, use****less****, bump****y****, danger****ous****, port****able***
adjectives of degree	Adjectives used to show how things compare with each other. *big, bigger, biggest; soft, softer, softest*
adverb	A word that says more about a verb, adjective or other adverb. *run* ***quickly****, it is* ***very*** *hot*
adverb of manner	A word that says **how** things happen. *walking* ***briskly****, strolling* ***slowly****, eating* ***greedily****, sleeping* ***quietly***
adverb of place	A word that says **where** things happen. *Sit* ***there****. Come* ***here****. Run* ***away****. It is lost* ***somewhere****.*
adverb of time	A word that says **when** things happen. *Go home* ***now****. He left* ***immediately****. You go, I'll come* ***later****.* A word that says **how often** or for **how long** things happen. *I go there* ***often****. He smiled* ***briefly****.*
adverb phrase	A group of words that does the work of an adverb. It says **how**, **where** and **when** things happen.
answer	A statement in reply to a question.
antonym	A word of opposite meaning. *big, little; long, short; hot, cold; happy, sad; beginning, end*
apostrophe	A punctuation mark used to show noun ownership and contractions ('). *Lyn's biro, Ben's dog, can't, won't, it's, she'll*
article	The words **a**, **an** and **the**. They introduce nouns and noun groups. ***a*** *cloudy, wet day;* ***an*** *egg;* ***the*** *cat*
auxiliary verb	A 'helper' verb. It works with another verb in a verb group. *They* ***are*** *skiing. I* ***can*** *sing. You* ***must*** *whisper.*
'be' verb	A verb that links ideas together. ***am, is, are, was, were, be, being, been***
body language	Our posture, gestures and facial expressions that show how we are thinking and feeling.

capital letter	An upper case letter used at the beginning of a sentence and a proper name. ***W**e were late. **I** gave **J**oe a pie.*
collective noun	A name given to a group of people or animals. *family, crowd, pack, mob, herd, flock*
comma	A punctuation mark used to separate words in a list, or to mark off a beginning phrase or a phrase in the middle of a sentence. (,) *Suddenly**,** a bear**,** a fox and a rabbit ran out of the woods. Mia**,** lost for words**,** could only gaze in wonder.*
command	A sentence giving an order or command. Its subject is understood to be **you**. *Turn off the light and go to sleep.*
common noun	A word that names everyday people, animals, places and things. *cup, teacher, dingo, phone*
compound noun	A word made by joining two words together. ***corn**flakes, **sea**side, **snow**ball, **cow**boy, **butter**fly*
compound sentence	Two (or more) simple sentences joined together by a **joining word**. *You make the bed **and** I'll sweep the floor.*
contractions	Two words shortened into one. **pronoun + helper:** *I'm, he's, they've;* **helper + not:** *can't, didn't, haven't*
count noun	A word that names things that can be counted. *chairs, boxes, bees, book, people, zebras*
definite article	The word **the**. It relates to a particular person or thing and tells people **who** or **what** is being spoken about. *a picture, an elephant*
demonstrative pronoun	The pronouns **this**, **that**, **these** and **those**. *May I have one of **those**? I'll take **these** with me. **This** belongs to me.*
'do' verb	A verb that shows some action being carried out. ***do, does, did, done***
doing verb	A verb that expresses action. *run, hop, skip, cook, read*
exclamation	A sentence that shows sudden excitement, surprise, fear or happiness, and ends with an exclamation mark. *I can't believe it! Hey! Wait for me!*
exclamation mark	A punctuation mark placed at the end of a written exclamation. (!) *Get out of the way**!** Go to bed, NOW**!***
fact	Something true that can be proven. *The meerkat belongs to the mongoose family. It lives in South Africa.*
first person	The person speaking. *Hi. My name is Jill. **I** have a friend called Jess. She likes to play hockey, but **I** like netball.*
first person pronoun	A pronoun used to tell a personal story. ***I, me, we, us***
full stop	A punctuation mark used to mark the end of a sentence. (.) *The sun sets in the west**.** Put your toys away, please**.***
future tense (verb)	A verb that talks about things that will happen in the future. Most use the helper **will**. *We **will leave** soon. **Will** you **wait**?*

gender noun	A name that is specific to a male or female. *girl, boy; man, woman; prince, princess; father, mother; king, queen*
grammar	The way our language is built through words, phrases and sentences.
'have' verb	A verb that shows ownership or action. ***has, have, had***
helper verb	An important word that forms part of a **verb** group. (Also called an auxiliary verb.) ***am, is, are, was, were, be, being, been, do, does, did, has, have, had, will***
indefinite article	The words **a** and **an**. They do not relate to any particular person or thing. ***the*** *red rose,* ***the*** *tall and handsome prince*
indefinite pronoun	A pronoun that refers to people and things in a general way. It is followed by a singular verb. ***someone, everybody, nothing, something***
infinitive	A word made up of **to + verb**. It answers the question **why** or **what**. *I like* ***to cook****. I went* ***to see*** *Grandma. I'm waiting for the sun* ***to set****. She comes over* ***to play*** *on Sundays.*
interrogative adverb	An adverb that asks a question. ***When*** *is your birthday?* ***How*** *far is it to Perth?* ***Where*** *did you put your coat?* ***Why*** *are you crying?*
interrogative pronoun	A pronoun used to ask a question. ***Who*** *is at the door?* ***What*** *is wrong?* ***Which*** *book did you read?* ***Whose*** *hat is this?*
irregular noun	A noun that has a special plural form. ***child****, children;* ***goose****, geese;* ***tooth****, teeth;* ***foot****, feet;* ***man****, men;* ***woman****, women*
irregular plural noun	A plural noun that has a special form. *child,* ***children****; goose,* ***geese****; tooth,* ***teeth****; foot,* ***feet****; man,* ***men****; woman,* ***women***
irregular verb	A verb that has its own past tense form. ***Draw:*** *I drew, I was drawing, I have drawn.* ***Sing:*** *I sang, I was singing, I have sung.*
joining word	A word that joins ideas together. ***and, but, so, or***
mass noun	A word that names something that cannot be counted. *rice, rain, snow, sand, salt*
modal adverb	An adverb that makes adjectives and other adverbs weaker or stronger. *She is* ***very*** *popular. They were* ***almost*** *ripe.*
modal verb	A helper that makes verbs weaker or stronger. *He* ***could*** *go. He* ***might*** *go. He* ***will*** *go. He* ***must*** *go. He* ***should*** *go.*
negative adverb	The adverbs **not** and **never**. *I am* ***never*** *coming back. The dog is* ***not*** *in its kennel. The bus* ***can't*** *wait.*
noun	A naming word. *Gerry, door, violin, car, house, sun, lion, jackal*
noun group	A group of words with the **noun** as the main word. ***my shiny red*** *shoes,* ***an old straw*** *hat,* ***the deep blue*** *sea*
object	A subject does the action. An **object** receives the action. *The boy hit* ***the ball****.*

opinion	A statement of what a person thinks about something. It may or may not be true. *Children watch too much TV.*
participle	A word that can be used as an adjective, often called a verbal adjective. It can be **present** (ending in **–ing**) or **past** (ending in **–ed**). *walking, sparkling, crumpled, spotted*
participle phrase	A phrase beginning with a participle. It works like an adjective. *I saw a boy **eating ice cream**. I saw a truck **loaded with coal**.*
passive verb	A **verb** that shows the subject being acted upon. *The fox **was chased** by the dog. The ball **was thrown** by the boy.*
passive voice	Voice refers to the kinds of verbs used. The **verb** (and voice) is passive when the subject is receiving the action. *The mouse **was chased** by the cat.*
past participle	A word that most often ends in **–ed.** It can be part of a verb group *(I **have baked** a cake)* or can be an adjective *(**baked** beans).*
past tense (time)	A way of showing that an event has taken place in the past. *I walked home from school yesterday.*
past tense (verb)	An event that has already happened. *They **won** the game. We **were lost** in the forest. They **swam** back to shore.*
person	The way pronouns are used to show who is speaking. First person: ***I, we***; Second person: ***you***; Third person: ***he, she, it, they***.
personal pronoun	A word that replaces the name of a person or thing. ***I, you, he, she, him, her, it, we, they, me, us, them***
phrase	A 'chunk' of words that go together. It has no verb and does not make sense on its own. *across the sea, in bed*
pitch	The rise and fall of our voice as we speak.
plural	A word that shows more than one person or thing.
plural noun	The name of more than one thing. *flowers, grapes, tigers, birds, donkeys, men, children*
plural pronoun	A pronoun that names more than one thing and replaces a plural noun. ***we, us, they, them, you***
plural subject	A subject that names more than one thing. *the children, some dogs, two women*
plural verb	A verb that says what more than one person or thing is doing. A plural **verb** must agree with a plural subject. *The boys **were reading**. The hens **are feeding**.*
possessive noun	A noun that names the owner of something. An apostrophe shows who the owner is. ***Jack's** hat, **girl's** basket, **birds'** nests, **babies'** bibs, **children's** clothes, **men's** trousers*
possessive pronoun	A pronoun that shows ownership. It does not need an apostrophe. *The book is **hers**. Is this ball **yours**?*

predicate	The part of a sentence that says what the subject is doing. It has a **verb**. *Dad* ***is driving*** *the car.*
preposition	A word that shows position and introduces a phrase. ***under, over, on, in, of, by***
preposition phrase	A phrase beginning with a preposition. ***under*** *the chair,* ***in*** *the cupboard,* ***in*** *the sink,* ***above*** *the clouds,* ***near*** *the door*
present participle	A word ending in **–ing**. It can be an adjective *(He has a* ***walking*** *stick)* or part of a verb group *(I* ***am walking*** *home).*
present tense (time)	A way of showing that an event is taking place at the present time. *I am reading this book.*
present tense (verb)	An event that is happening now. It can be simple *(I* ***wash*** *my hands. The owl* ***hunts*** *mice.)* or continuous *(I* ***am washing*** *my hands. The owl* ***is hunting*** *mice.).*
pronoun	A word that takes the place of a noun. *Jack,* ***he****; children,* ***they****; girl,* ***she****; basket,* ***it***
pronoun reference	Pronouns refer to the nouns they replace. They usually refer backwards. *The* ***box*** *is on the table.* ***It*** *is big.*
proper noun	The name of a particular person, thing or event. It begins with a capital letter. *Toby, Perth, April, Easter, Swan River*
punctuation	A marking system that writers use to help readers make meaning from their words.
question	A sentence that asks for information and ends with a question mark. An answer is usually expected. *Have you read this book? Did you win?*
question mark	A punctuation mark (**?**) placed at the end of a question. *Are you watching***?** *Do you like pasta***?**
reflexive pronoun	A pronoun that refers to the subject. *Bob did it* ***himself****. I hurt* ***myself****. We saw* ***ourselves*** *in the mirror. (you) Get it* ***yourself****.*
regular verb	A verb that has **–s** or **–es**, **–ing**, or **–ed** added to it to form present and past tense. *plays, play****ing****, play****ed****; listens, listen****ed****, listen****ing***
second person	The person spoken to (you). *Did* ***you*** *say* ***you*** *were going to the beach? Don't forget* ***your*** *hat and* ***your*** *sunscreen.*
second person pronoun	A pronoun used when people are speaking to each other. ***you***
sentence	A 'chunk' of language that makes sense on its own. It is a complete thought. *They are ice skating.*
simple sentence	A sentence with a subject and a **verb**. *The cows* ***were milked****.* ***Can*** *you* ***cook?*** *A rooster* ***crows****.*
simple verb	A one-word verb. *licks, spoke, like, lost*
singular	A word that shows one person or thing.
singular noun	The name of one thing. *toy, bike, pig, tree, street, planet*

singular pronoun	A pronoun that names one thing and replaces a singular noun. ***I, me, he, him, she, her, you, it***
singular subject	A subject that names one thing. *James, a dog, my sister, the yellow bus*
singular verb	A verb that says what one person or thing is doing. A singular **verb** must agree with a singular subject. *The ball* ***is rolling****.* *I* ***am eating.***
speech marks	Punctuation marks (" ") used in writing to show spoken words. *"Would you like an ice cream?" asked Jill. "Yes please," I said.*
spoken language	A language where people use their voices to express what they want to say.
statement	A sentence that states facts or ideas. *The sun is hot. Eva has a black horse.*
subject	A subject says **who** or **what** a sentence is about. *Our football team won the game. Ms Jett is a doctor.*
subject-verb agreement	A singular subject has a singular **verb**. *He* ***is playing*** *chess.* A plural subject has a plural **verb**. *They* ***are playing*** *chess.*
suffix	A syllable attached to the end of a word to change the way the word is used. *great**ness**, care**ful**, anxious**ly***
tense (verb)	Verbs say when things happen. Tense refers to the point in time that things are happening. ***Present:*** *I am running.* ***Past:*** *I ran.* ***Future:*** *I will run.*
third person	The people and things being spoken about. ***Ted*** *has a lot of marbles.* ***He*** *takes* ***them*** *to school and plays with his friends.*
third person pronoun	A pronoun used when speaking about other people and things. ***he, him, she, her, it, them, they***
verb	A word that says what people and things are **doing**, **saying**, **thinking** or **feeling**. *I* ***am hopping****. He* ***shouted****. I* ***believe*** *you.*
verb group	A group of words containing two or more verbs. *I* ***can hop*** *on one leg. Jane* ***will go*** *for a walk soon.*
verbal adjective	A present or past participle used as an adjective. ***walking*** *stick,* ***falling*** *snow,* ***baked*** *beans,* ***puzzled*** *look*
visual language	Information received from pictures, photos, posters, movies etc.
voice	Refers to the kinds of verbs used. **active verbs/voice:** the subject is doing the action; **passive verbs/voice:** the subject is receiving the action.
written language	A language where people use written words and marks to express what they want to say.

INDEX